CUBA: A SHORT HISTORY

The following titles drawn from
The Cambridge History of Latin America edited by Leslie Bethell
are available in hardcover and paperback:

Colonial Spanish America

Colonial Brazil

The Independence of Latin America

Spanish America after Independence, *c.* 1820 – *c.* 1870

Brazil: Empire and Republic, 1822–1930

Latin America: Economy and Society, 1870–1930

Mexico since Independence

Central America since Independence

Cuba: A Short History

Chile since Independence

Argentina since Independence

CUBA:
A SHORT HISTORY

edited by
LESLIE BETHELL
Professor of Latin American History
University of London

CAMBRIDGE
UNIVERSITY PRESS

PUBLISHED BY THE PRESS SYNDICATE OF THE UNIVERSITY OF CAMBRIDGE
The Pitt Building, Trumpington Street, Cambridge CB2 1RP, United Kingdom

CAMBRIDGE UNIVERSITY PRESS
The Edinburgh Building, Cambridge CB2 2RU, UK   http: //www.cup.cam.ac.uk
40 West 20th Street, New York, NY 10011-4211, USA   http: //www.cup.org
10 Stamford Road, Oakleigh, Melbourne 3166, Australia

First published 1993
Reprinted 1993, 1994, 1995, 1996 (twice), 1998

Printed in the United States of America

The contents of this book were previously published as parts of
volumes III, V and VII of *The Cambridge History of Latin America,*
copyright © Cambridge University Press 1985, 1986, 1990.

Typeset in Garamond

A catalogue record for this book is available from the British Library

Library of Congress Cataloguing-in-Publication Data is available

ISBN 0-521-43063-1 hardback
ISBN 0-521-43682-6 paperback

CONTENTS

PREFACE

The Cambridge History of Latin America is a large scale, collaborative, multi-volume history of Latin America during the five centuries from the first contacts between Europeans and the native peoples of the Americas in the late fifteenth and early sixteenth centuries to the present.

Cuba: A Short History brings together chapters from Volumes III, V and VII of *The Cambridge History* to provide in a single volume an economic, social and political history of Cuba since the middle of the eighteenth century. This, it is hoped, will be useful for both teachers and students of Latin American history and of contemporary Latin America. Each chapter is accompanied by a bibliographical essay.

1

CUBA, *c.* 1750–*c.* 1860

The Spanish colony of Cuba in the mid-eighteenth century was a largely forested, half unmapped island. It was known both to Spaniards and their enemies among other European empires primarily as the hinterland to Havana. That famous port had been built in the 1560s in a natural harbour on the north of the island to act as a depot from whence the Spanish treasure fleet could pick up a large naval escort. The few intrepid travellers who penetrated into the interior would have observed that the fauna of Cuba was friendly: there were no snakes, few big reptiles and no large wild animals. The indigenous Indian population – Tainos or Ciboneys – was held to have been absorbed or had died out, though in the unfrequented East of the island a few Taino villages survived. Some 'white' Spanish (or *criollo*) families had some Indian blood – including the Havana grandees, the Recios de Oquendo family.

About half the Cuban population of 150,000 or so lived in the city of Havana, where malaria and yellow fever frequently raged. Most of the rest lived in a few other towns, such as Santiago de Cuba, the seat of an archbishop, Puerto Príncipe, which boasted a bishopric, Sancti Spiritus, Trinidad, Matanzas and Mariel. None of these reached 10,000 in population. Rising above these cities, or near them, were a number of sixteenth-century castles and churches. In Havana three fortresses – la Fuerza, el Morro and la Punta – had all been built to guard the port. Communications were mostly, as elsewhere in the Spanish Americas, by sea. There were few roads. The only substantial employer was the royal dockyard at Havana under the Spanish captain-general and, in order to guarantee to him a ready supply of tropical hardwoods, the felling of all such hardwood trees in the island was supposed to be controlled.

There was little industry in Cuba besides ship repairing, the curing of pork, the salting of beef and the tanning of leather, all of which was done for the benefit of the convoys from Veracruz and Portobelo. There had once in the sixteenth century been a little gold in Cuban rivers, but what there was had been recovered long ago. In Cuba in 1750 there were about a hundred small sugar plantations, mostly close to Havana: the cost of carrying sugar to any other port was prohibitive. They were customarily powered by a handful of oxen. They probably produced about 5,000 tons of sugar a year of which only a tenth was officially exported. In comparison, the territorially much smaller French and English sugar colonies, such as Saint-Domingue or Jamaica, had about six hundred larger plantations which could produce 250 tons of sugar each.

This backwardness in Cuba derived partly from the fact that the island had few rivers suitable to power water mills which were responsible for the wealth of other colonies in the Caribbean. It was partly also because there was no large-scale home market in Spain for such a luxury as sugar.

Tobacco was Cuba's most profitable crop. Much of it was made into snuff, though tobacco planters had already established their *vegas* in the valley of the River Cuyaguateje in West Cuba and begun to plant there the tobacco which later made a 'Havana cigar' the jewel of the smoking world. Not till after 1770 were there any cigar factories in Cuba: cigars were for generations rolled on the spot by the pickers of the tobacco, or the leaf was sent back to Spain to Seville for *cigarros*. Tobacco farms were small in size, as were those which concentrated on bee-keeping for beeswax – another modest export. A few ranches in the savannah of central Cuba produced leather and beef; indeed, prior to the development of snuff, cattle-breeding and the production of hides had been Cuba's main export.

The native Indians of the sixteenth century also passed on to the Spaniards the art of cultivating sweet potato, yam, yucca, pumpkin, maize and various beans, though the colonists avoided vegetables and preferred to import almost everything which they had to eat: bread, for instance, was as a rule made from imported wheat. Wine, too, was imported not made. Fish was not much enjoyed. Coffee had begun to be grown in the French West Indies, but none had yet been introduced into Cuba – or for that matter into any Spanish colony.

Political control of Cuba lay with the captain-general, who himself ultimately depended on the viceroy in Mexico. But Mexico was several weeks away, Spain at least six weeks. The captain-general in Havana also had to share responsibility *de facto* with the commander of the treasure fleet while the latter was in Havana for about six weeks a year. The

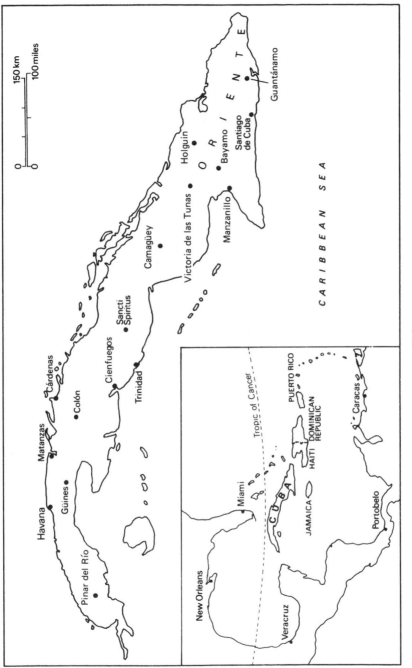

Cuba

captain-general was the father of a small bureaucracy of officials who had been appointed to their posts by the home administrators in Seville. Most of these, like the captain-general himself, were badly paid. All hoped for profit from graft out of their official posts. Treasurers, accountants, judges, naval commissars and port officials of every kind came as poor *peninsulares* to the Spanish empire, as did bishops and priests, and expected one day to return rich to Andalusia or to Castile. But many such persons never in fact returned home and left their families to swell the class of *criollos* who managed the town councils, established prices for most basic commodities, farmed and often eventually became merchants or landowners.

Cuba like the rest of the Spanish empire had by the eighteenth century its own *criollo* aristocracy which consisted of a handful of rich families of whom some – Recio de Oquendo, Herrera, Núñez del Castillo, Calvo de la Puerta and Beltrán de la Cruz – had been in the island for several generations. They would customarily live most of the year in town houses, in Havana (or perhaps Santiago, or Trinidad), visit their plantations or ranches at harvest or times of religious festivals and, as a rule, never visit Spain or any other part of the empire. In this respect they differed from those absentee landlords who enriched themselves in the rest of the Caribbean. These Cuban oligarchs are more to be compared with their cousins on the mainland in this as in other respects.

Three other things distinguished Cuba from many non-Spanish colonies in the Caribbean: the relatively small number of slaves; the relatively large number of free blacks and mulattos; and the importance of urban life. The sugar plantations of the British and French colonies, like those of Portuguese Brazil, had demanded vast numbers of slaves. The smaller number of small-sized Cuban plantations needed fewer. In 1750, there were probably more slaves in Havana in private houses, shipyards or on cattle ranches than there were on sugar plantations. Freed negroes constituted almost a third of the black or mulatto population of the city of Havana. This high proportion was partly the consequence of explicit laws making the purchase of liberty by slaves easier than in, say, British colonies. Partly it derived from the presence of a ruling class willing to emancipate slaves on their death bed – and specially willing to emancipate their bastards. The social and political structure of the island of Cuba, like that of the rest of the Spanish empire, had led to the creation of cities. The English colonies in the Caribbean had scarcely any urban life and that went for English North America as well.

During the second half of the eighteenth century Cuba was transformed into a prosperous sugar colony. These were the four main causes:
first, the creation of a new market for sugar at home in Spain and
elsewhere – including the newly independent United States of America;
secondly the emergence of a class of landlords interested in developing
their land and promoting wealth, rather than in preserving status;
thirdly, the import of slaves from Africa to Cuba on a far larger scale than
before; and finally a series of far-reaching economic reforms introduced
by the enlightened ministers of King Charles III, not least the lifting of
many of the old bureaucratic restraints on trade. The gradual decline of
other islands in the Caribbean as sugar producers also contributed to
Cuba's prosperity. More and more investors from outside the Spanish
empire put money into Cuba to the benefit both of themselves and of the
island, and the colony was quick to introduce new technology in the
sugar industry.

The event around which these developments revolved was the British
occupation of Havana in 1762. We should not fear to designate turning
points in history, if the events really justify it – as these do. The victory of
Lord Albemarle's expedition to west Cuba was, of course, first and
foremost the conclusion of a victorious war for Britain. Havana had
never fallen before to foreign invaders. The British victory was the signal
for an immediate descent on the island by merchants of all sorts from all
parts of the British Empire – sellers of grain, horses, cloth and woollen
goods, iron-ware and minor industrial equipment, sugar equipment and
slaves. Before 1762, the Cuban market had been formally closed to
foreigners, although much smuggling had occurred.

The chief consequence of Albemarle's victory was that, during the
year when the English directed the affairs of Havana, about 4,000 slaves
were sold there. This figure was perhaps equivalent to one-eighth of the
number of slaves in the island at that time. Earlier applications under
Spain to expand the import of slaves had been rejected by the government in Havana on the ground that it would be politically risky to have so
many new slaves (*bozales*) in the island. Such fears were now shown to be
over-cautious. No great slave revolt followed the sudden increase. When
the British left the island after the peace of Paris (1763), slave factors and
mercantile relationships with the British islands remained. During the
eighteen years following 1763, the number of ships calling per year in
Cuba rose from 6 to 200. In particular, there was a steady increase in
imports of slaves into Cuba, many of them re-exported from Jamaica.

Slave monopolies granted to particular companies lasted another generation but were evaded. British and North American dealers were a
permanent feature in the Cuban market, and after 1775 Spanish merchants began to go to Africa to bring back slaves to Havana – many of
them being re-sold elsewhere in the empire. In 1778 the Spanish purchased Fernando Po and Annobon from Portugal. In 1789, the Spanish
Government permitted merchants to bring into the empire as many
slaves as they liked – the only regulation being that a third of each
shipload had to be women.

    Another immediate consequence of the British conquest was the
disappearance of most old Spanish taxes – *almojarifazgos* (payable on all
goods coming in from Spain); *averia* (payable to the navy); *alcabalas*
(payable on all exports to Spain); and *donativos* (extra levies paid on
demand to help the government in Madrid). Some of these, it is true,
were temporarily restored after the British left. But most restrictions on
trade were abolished for good. In 1765, the right of Spaniards to trade in
the Caribbean was extended to other ports than Cadiz – seven, to begin
with – but that really meant that anyone in Spain who wanted to trade
with Cuba could do so, for the ports included Barcelona, Malaga,
Alicante, Corunna and Santander – a broad spectrum. Commercial
activity within the Spanish empire was free by the time of the War of
American Independence. In 1771 the unstable local copper coinage, the
macuquina, was replaced by the *peso fuerte*. In 1776 Havana became a free
port. Further, the regulation of commerce within the Spanish empire, in
Cuba as in Venezuela, ceased to be the business of the local town council.
The interest of the crown was secured, in the empire as in Spain, by a
general financial commissioner, *intendente*, whose effectiveness was considerable. He enabled the Spanish crown to gain more income from fairer
taxes – an ideal fiscal achievement. In the 1790s duties on the import of
machinery for the production of sugar or coffee were similarly abandoned. Foreign merchants were not only permitted to enter and to settle
in the island but were allowed to buy property; so both British and
United States merchants were soon to be found well-established there.

    Francisco de Arango, a planter and lawyer who had fought in the
courts of Madrid, successfully, against the suggestion that the last slave
monopoly (granted to the English firm of Baker and Dawson) should be
renewed, travelled to England with his fellow sugar planter and distant
relation, the conde de Casa Montalvo, to see how the merchants in
Liverpool and London ran their slave trade and how English manufac-

turers worked their factories. On their return to Cuba in 1792 they founded the *Sociedad Económica de Amigos del País*, in Havana, on the model of similar societies elsewhere in Spain and the Spanish empire. That body inspired governmental enquiries and the gathering of both statistics and economic information, and it also led indirectly to the foundation of Cuba's first rudimentary newspaper, *El Papel Periódico*, a daily newsheet from 1793.

Arango and his generation were pioneers of every kind of innovation. They created a public library, built hospitals, a lunatic asylum and free schools (for white children only). In England, Arango had looked at, and been impressed by, a steam engine. One was taken to Cuba in 1794 by the Reinhold firm to be used experimentally in 1797 at the conde de Casa Montalvo's son-in-law's plantation, at Seybabo. Water mills were also used successfully for the first time in west Cuba after French planters and technicians fleeing from the Haitian Revolution had brought to Cuba the idea of the overshot water wheel. Another innovation of the 1790s was a dumb turner which took the place of slaves introducing the cane into the wheel of the mill. A new sugar cane was introduced too in the 1790s – the strong South Sea 'otaheite' strain, while – probably equally important – mangoes were brought to supplement the meagre fruit diet by an English merchant, Philip Allwood, the powerful and controversial representative in Havana of the big Liverpool firm of slave merchants, Baker and Dawson.

By the turn of the eighteenth and the nineteenth century, therefore, Cuba was plainly a very promising part of the Spanish empire, bidding fair, with its plantations spreading far away from Havana, to overtake Jamaica as the biggest producer of sugar in the Caribbean. Spain gave every fiscal encouragement both to those producing and exporting sugar and to those seeking an adequate slave labour force. The export of sugar from Cuba by 1800 already exceeded that of hides, tobacco, cane brandy, wax, coffee and nuts which also came into Spain in ships from Havana. Thus, in the 1770s, Cuba was exporting over 10,000 tons of sugar a year and in the 1790s, just before the outbreak of the Napoleonic Wars, over 30,000 tons. The number of plantations growing sugar increased from about 100 to about 500, and the land planted to sugar cane had increased from 10,000 acres to nearly 200,000. The average size of a sugar plantation in 1762 in Cuba was probably no more than 300 acres; by the 1790s, it was nearly 700. Whereas many old sugar plantations had employed barely a dozen slaves, many new ones of the 1790s employed 100.

As in all progress which involves an increase in the scale of operations, there was an element of suffering. Bigger plantations meant more remote landlords. Mulattos or freed slaves ceased to own sugar mills – as they had occasionally done before 1760. More slaves meant bigger dwelling places, barracks taking the place of huts, and hence fewer private plots on which a slave in the early eighteenth century might have kept a chicken or planted cassava for bread. Small mills vanished, or ceased to make real sugar, producing instead only *raspadura* or rough sugar for consumption by the slaves themselves. Fewer and fewer sugar plantations remained self-sufficient, able to grow maize and vegetables, as well as sugar, burning their own wood or eating their own cattle. Few plantations too troubled about carrying out the Church's regulations that all slaves should be instructed in Christianity. New sugar mills increasingly had lay rather than religious names. Priests turned a blind eye to work on Sundays, and slaves were often buried in unconsecrated ground. Even so, monasteries and even the seminary of Havana in the 1790s had their sugar mills.

Another element had by now also entered Cuban history – and one which has since never been wholly absent: namely, the world sugar market, that is to say, the interests of rich consumers of sugar in other countries. 'I know not why we should blush to confess it', wrote John Adams, 'but molasses was an essential ingredient in American independence'. For two generations before 1775, Massachusetts had drunk, and profited from selling, the best 'Antilles rum'. Jamaica could no longer satisfy the needs of the rum merchants of Massachusetts, since its production was falling, with its soil exhausted. Farmers and planters alike in that era were ignorant of the benefits of fertilizer. North American merchants desired, therefore, to trade with both French and Spanish sugar colonies before the war of independence. British regulations prevented them from doing so. Symbolic of the importance of the Cuban trade in North American eyes was the nomination as first United States commercial representative in Cuba of Robert Smith, the representative in Havana of Robert Morris, the financier of the American Revolution. Most of the increase of sugar production in Cuba was soon being sold in the United States.

The revolution in Haiti (Saint-Domingue) had, if anything, an even greater consequence for Cuba than did the American Revolution. The slave revolt first of all increased the demand for Cuban sugar in such a way as greatly to please Arango and his colleagues. Sugar prices rose so as to increase the tendency, anyway great, of Cuban landowners to turn over their land to sugar cane. But the revolution in Haiti also caused tremors of fear to run through all the plantations of Cuba. Haiti might be ruined commercially after 1791, and that might benefit Cuba economically. But the danger was that the ruin might spread – or be spread. After all, several of the revolutionaries in Saint-Domingue had been Jamaican or had come from elsewhere in the West Indies.

In the event, it was the French planters – those who could do so – who fled from Haiti to Cuba and elsewhere in the still safe Caribbean. And they brought not only terrible stories of murder and revolution but also many useful techniques, to add to those already recently put into use, for the cultivation and processing of sugar. The most important were, first, the so-called 'Jamaican train', by which a long train of copper cauldrons could be heated over a single fire at the same time and at the same temperature and, secondly, the overshot water-wheels which have already been mentioned. Sugar technicians who had worked in Haiti, many born in France, were soon found on the bigger Cuban plantations.

International connections, however, spelled international troubles as well as wealth. The Napoleonic wars not only interrupted trade and delayed the introduction of steam engines for the mills of Cuba on any large scale but also gave the planters an experience of wild fluctuations in sugar prices. In 1807, two-thirds of the sugar harvest went unsold because of a sudden United States suppression of trade with all belligerents. In 1808, the collapse of the Spanish crown before Napoleon left the captain-general, the marqués de Someruelos, with virtually full power in Cuba. The island was in an exposed strategic position. That in turn caused President Jefferson to make the first of many United States bids to protect the island: the United States, he said, would prefer Cuba – and Mexico – to remain Spanish but, should Spain not be able to maintain it herself, the United States would be willing to buy the island. The offer was turned down, but Jefferson continued to toy with the idea while the *cabildo* in Havana, led by Francisco de Arango's cousin, José de Arango, made some moves to suggest annexation to the United States in the face of what some members took to be dangerously liberal tendencies in Spain itself, especially with respect to the abolition of slavery.

The Napoleonic wars were, of course, the midwife of Latin American independence. Cut off from the *madre patria* by the destruction of the Spanish fleet at Trafalgar, enriched by the last thirty years of the Bourbon economic reformation, and politically stimulated by the American, as

well as the French, revolutions, *criollos* in South America everywhere
began to contemplate political autonomy, even formal independence
from Spain. Such ideas, blending with or transforming revolutionary
ideas from Haiti, naturally reached Cuba also: a freemason, Ramón de la
Luz, organized one of those romantic and ineffective conspiracies which
characterized the novels of Stendhal or the history of the Risorgimento
in Italy in order to achieve Cuban independence in 1809. These ideas did
not prosper, however, for a simple reason: the spectre of Haiti. No sane
Cuban planter was ready to risk a serious quarrel with Spain and the
Spanish garrison if there were the remotest danger of the opportunity
being exploited by leaders of a successful slave revolt. Hence the *junta
superior* of Havana rejected the invitation of the *cabildo* of Caracas to take
part in the wars of independence. Some physical impediments also
restrained Cubans. Cuba was an island and the loyalty to Spain of its cities
could easily be maintained by only a few ships of the fleet – should one
ever be assembled. Then many royalist refugees fled or emigrated to
Cuba from various parts of the Spanish empire on the mainland –
strengthening Cuba's reputation as the 'ever faithful island'. Finally, the
priests in Cuba, unlike those on the mainland, were mostly Spanish-born,
and had no ambition to echo the exploits of the fathers Hidalgo and
Morelos in Mexico. Still, it was probably the fear of 'a new Haiti' that
most restrained the Cubans: an anxiety given weight by the discovery of
another romantic conspiracy – this time led by José Antonio Aponte, a
negro carpenter, who planned to burn cane and coffee fields, who
apparently made contact with co-religionaries in Haiti and who invoked
the African god Chango to help him. A later conspiracy, the *Soles y Rayos
de Bolívar* headed by José Francisco Lemus in the 1820s, was much more
formidable but, like Aponte's, was also betrayed in the end.

At the same time the Cuban planters were concerned at the threat
posed by the British campaign to abolish the slave trade internationally,
following the ban on the trade to and from British ports (introduced in
1808). Francisco Arango and others had spoken forcefully against any
concessions on this front whilst in Spain in 1812 and 1813, and the first
Spanish government after the restoration of Ferdinand VII in 1814 at
first resisted British demands. But in 1817 the British were successful in
persuading Spain formally to follow their example, and in 1820 Spain
legally abolished the slave trade in return for £400,000, to be paid as
compensation to slave merchants. Spain also accepted the right of the
Royal Navy to stop slave ships and to bring suspected slavers for trial

before mixed commissions. This measure naturally led to an increase in slave imports during what seemed in Havana likely to be the last years of the trade. But the ban was not carried out – however much the English began to accustom Cubans to the idea of international intervention in their affairs. The demand for slaves was great and growing and, with ups and downs, the trade survived another fifty years, not least because the government in Madrid was unwilling to antagonize the planters of Cuba by supporting the British whom they believed to be sanctimonious, hypocritical and self-seeking.

As early as 1822, partly in consequence of this British interference, planters in Cuba began to explore again the idea of joining the United States as a new state of the Union. The United States Cabinet discussed the idea but sought to dissuade the Cubans. They preferred the status quo. Yet most leading Americans then supposed that Cuban adhesion to their Union was only a matter of time – a generation at most. Certainly therefore they did not wish to see the independence of the island.

Various schemes for both independence or annexation were widely discussed in the *tertulias* in Havana cafés in the mid-1820s. But, in the event, having lost her mainland American empire, Spain was determined to keep Cuba and Puerto Rico. Forty thousand Spanish troops were stationed in Cuba from the 1820s onwards. They and a network of government spies preserved the island's loyalty. Bolívar once contemplated an invasion of Cuba if the Spaniards did not recognize his new Colombia. The United States were discouraging, and the moment passed.

Cuba's political docility, guaranteed by the Spanish garrison, was the frame for a rapid increase of prosperity based on sugar, as we shall see. By the 1830s Cuba's taxes produced a substantial revenue for the Spanish crown. Cuban revenues were popularly held to account for the salaries of most Spanish ministers. They gave the only guarantee for repayment of debt that could be offered by Spanish governments to London bankers. The captains-general in Cuba profited too – partly from bribes which were the consequence of winking at the slave trade. And this often enabled them to pursue ambitious political programmes at home in Spain on retirement. Had the captains-general fulfilled their obligations and undertaken to abolish the slave trade they would have lost the colony – but to the United States rather than to an independence movement. The old social gap between *criollos* and *peninsulares* persisted. Forbidden to take part in administration – and there was, after all, no politics – the

criollos grumbled and made money instead. The slightest hint that
Spanish control might be relaxed, or that a slave revolt might get out of
hand, suggested to Cuba's landowners that the time might come when
they should join the North American union. Planters were usually made
happy by the determination of successive captains-general, who deported progressive or nationalist writers regularly and who successfully
avoided implementing in Cuba the sporadic lurches towards constitutional rule in Spain. The largest sugar mills founded in the 1840s were
sometimes exposed to rebellions by slaves. They were put down with a
ruthlessness which the planters in Cuba feared would not be approached
by the United States government.

In the end, however, the idea of annexation to the Union seized the
imagination of a high proportion of prominent Cuban planters led by
Carlos Núñez del Castillo, Miguel Aldama, Cristóbal Madán and the
Iznaga and Drake families. Their purpose was to join the United States in
order to preserve slavery and to safeguard the pursuit of wealth through
sugar. They set themselves the task of persuading United States opinion
of their point of view. After the entry of Florida, Louisiana, Texas and
then (after 1848) California and New Mexico into the Union, Cuba
seemed the next obvious candidate. The idea also attracted the new
generation of North American politicians, stimulated by these other
territorial acquisitions, and intoxicated by the general success and
prosperity of the United States. Writers and journalists of the late 1840s
had a definite sense that it was 'manifest destiny', in the words of one of
them, that the United States should dominate, if not conquer, all the
Americas, south as well as north. A campaign urging the United States to
buy Cuba was launched. It was evident that many rich Cubans supported
the idea, and would do so, if need be, with their money. 'Cuba by
geographical position and right . . . must be ours', wrote the editor of the
New York Sun in 1847; it was 'the garden of the world'.

The annexation of Cuba constituted an important item in the presidential election of 1848. President Polk responded by agreeing to make a
formal offer for Cuba to Spain of $100 million. The idea was seriously
discussed in Spain but leaked – and uproar ensued. The Spanish government had to reject the idea in order to remain in office. Still, annexationist
ideas survived. An expedition of 'liberation' headed by a rebel Spanish
general, Narciso López, was prepared in New Orleans in 1849, and
eventually set off for Cuba in 1850, with the intention, first, of proclaim-
ing independence from Spain and, then, of joining the Union. The

scheme was betrayed, and López was captured and publicly garrotted, though López's flag – a single white star on a red background, the whole set against blue stripes – survived to inspire another generation of more genuine seekers after independence.

Other expeditions followed. The idea of annexation burned increasingly in the minds of the politicians of the U.S. South. The acquisition of Cuba would inevitably strengthen the slave states. For much of the 1850s, Cuban liberation represented one of the dreams of Young America, the proponents of the secession of the South, as indeed it did of romantic revolutionaries in Europe. Garibaldi, Mazzini and Kossuth, for instance, all added their weight to this essentially ambiguous cause. For their part, the planters in Cuba, even after the re-assuring pronouncements of Captain-General Pezuela in 1853, continued to fear that abolitionism might capture the minds of the Spanish officials.

Another offer was made to buy Cuba from Spain by President Pierce in 1854. Again it was rejected by a new government of liberals in Madrid. The Cuban planters were despondent. They feared that Spanish liberalism would be underwritten by English sanctimoniousness and thus permit the establishment of what they termed 'an African republic'. New efforts were made to secure United States interest – and, if necessary, intervention. James Buchanan, ex-secretary of state and minister in London in 1854, believed that, if Spain were to turn down the United States' 'reasonable' offers for Cuba, the United States would be 'justified in wresting it from her'. The Ostend manifesto between Buchanan, Pierce, Soulé (the United States minister in Madrid) and the United States minister in Paris denounced all plans which would lead to Cuba being 'Africanized', but it was disowned in Washington. In New Orleans, meantime, another expedition to liberate Cuba had been assembled under the governor of Louisiana, John Quitman; its members fell out among themselves. In 1857 James Buchanan became president of the United States, and his election owed much to the popularity of the manifesto of Ostend. Buchanan set about seeking to bribe Spanish politicians to sell Cuba – with no more success than had attended the efforts of his predecessors. The United States slid into civil war in 1861 at a moment when the politicians of the South still hoped that they could secure the perpetuation of slavery by acquiring Cuba. The defeat of the South closed that avenue for Cuban planters as it also closed the slave trade. The American Civil War was thus for Cuba the most important event since 1815.

Cuba, in the meantime, had become since the Napoleonic wars the richest colony in the world (which in part explains the limited extent of the psychological or intellectual stock-taking in Spain after the loss of the other provinces of the Spanish empire in the 1820s). Havana, with a population of nearly 200,000, and Santiago de Cuba were, by the 1860s, bustling cosmopolitan cities, while eight other towns had populations of over 10,000. Cuban ports received 3,600 ships a year of which half went to ports outside Havana. As early as 1825 the United States had become a more important trading partner for the colony than Spain; North Americans, merchants as well as politicians, had shown great interest in the island, investing in it and buying increasing percentages of Cuba's export crops.

For a time, coffee had made an effective challenge to sugar as Cuba's main export crop. Coffee had been introduced as early as 1748, but it was never grown on any scale till after the revolution in Haiti which brought to Cuba many experienced coffee growers. Some of those established themselves in Cuba and took full advantage of the tax exemptions which were designed to assist the growing of coffee. Between 1825 and 1845 exports of coffee from Cuba never fell below 12,000 tons, and land sown with coffee was in the mid-1840s slightly larger in extent than that sown with cane. But the rewards of coffee never seriously rivalled sugar, and in the 1850s many cafetals were turned into sugar plantations. The United States' tariffs on coffee imports of 1834, the terrible hurricanes of the 1840s and the beginning of Brazilian competition all damaged Cuban coffee interests. Coffee, however, remained an important crop till the beginning of the wars of independence. In 1860 there were still about 1,000 cafetals, producing 8,000 tons of coffee, mostly in East Cuba. Further hurricanes impoverished many coffee planters and stimulated the sense of deprivation which helped to create the rebellious mood in that region in the late 1860s.

Tobacco had also been a modest, but consistent, rival of sugar. The turning point in its history was the abolition of the royal monopoly of the manufacture of cigars in 1817. In 1821, the old royal tobacco factory – a building of the 1770s – was turned into a military hospital. Afterwards tobacco factories began gradually to be built chiefly by immigrants from Spain, such as Ramón Larrañaga and Ramón Allones. Cuban cigars were increasingly prized – though the majority of tobacco *vegas* continued to be in East Cuba not West, where the best tobacco was already known to be established. Another Cuban export was rum, the best marketed to great effect by Facundo Bacardí, a Catalan immigrant in the 1830s and a millionaire by the 1860s: his light amber product was a great international success.

Sugar remained, however, far and away Cuba's most important crop throughout the nineteenth century. In 1860, about $185 million were invested in sugar, the mills numbered 1,400 and Cuban production already reached some 450,000 tons – a quarter of the world's sugar, far above Jamaica, with only 148,000 tons during the 1850s. Steam-engines from England had been first introduced into sugar plantations during the second decade of the century (four were used in the harvest of 1818), and large steam-powered mills were now producing about 1,000 tons of sugar a year, in comparison with ox-powered mills which still averaged 130 tons only. A series of concessions by the Spanish crown had authorized the outright purchase of all land previously held in usufruct from the crown. The royal approval was also given to the destruction of hardwood forests in the interests of agriculture. A new sugar plantation area opened up in the 1820s and 1830s in Matanzas province at the mouth of the rivers San Juan and Yumurí between Matanzas itself, Colón and Cárdenas, and most of the steam mills were to be found there. The biggest sugar mill in Cuba in 1860 was *San Martín*, in Matanzas. It belonged to a company whose chief investor had apparently been the queen mother of Spain. It employed 800 slaves, planted 1,000 acres and produced 2,670 tons of sugar each year.

As early as 1845 the advanced sugar mills were all linked by private railway to Havana – an innovation which greatly lowered the cost of transporting cane. Cuba had the first railways in Latin America and the Caribbean: that between Havana and Bejucal was opened in 1837, that between Havana and Güines in 1838. In 1830, the average cost of carrying a box containing 3 or 4 cwt of sugar was estimated at $12.50. By train this had dropped after 1840 to $1.25. In the 1820s steam boats appeared too. A regular service plied between Havana and Matanzas as early as any such service in Europe. Steam-powered ships also ran between Havana and New Orleans in the 1830s. Other technological innovations in Cuba in the mid-nineteenth century included the vacuum boiler – first used in Cuba in 1835. The advanced vacuum boiler invented by Charles Derosne in Paris on the basis of the ideas of Norbert Rillieux created what was in effect a 'sugar machine' to co-ordinate all aspects of the manufacturing process. This was first installed in Cuba in 1841, by Derosne in person on the plantation *La Mella*, belonging to Wenceslao

Villa-Urrutia. The result was greatly to reduce the dependence of sugar makers on slaves. The Derosne mills could also produce a new and iridescent white sugar which was much sought after. Finally, in 1850 a centrifugal machine was introduced to Cuba on the mill called *Amistad*, belonging to Joaquín de Ayesterán. This enabled the sugar planter to convert the juice of the sugar cane into a clear, loose, dry and fine sugar in place of old sugar loaves immediately after it left the rollers. These technological developments increased the wealth of those who could afford them but depressed further those planters still using old ox-powered mills and, indeed, helped to drive them into rebellion.

The planters who did enjoy this new wealth were of three sorts: first, those, perhaps of recent Spanish (or Basque) origin, who had made fortunes in trading, particularly slave trading, and had either invested their profits in plantations or had acquired properties by foreclosing on debts. These were the men responsible for putting into effect most of the technological innovations of the age. The best known was Julián de Zulueta, the biggest proprietor in Cuba in the 1860s. Secondly, there were those who derived their sugar plantations from original grants from the Spanish crown in the eighteenth century or earlier, and who were in effect the aristocracy of the island. These families were deeply inter-related and had monopolized municipal government in Havana for a hundred years. Thirdly, there were already a number of foreigners, chiefly Americans, but also Englishmen and Frenchmen – of whom some became hispanicized (or cubanized) after a generation or so on the island. Some of each category became rich on an international level, secured Spanish titles, travelled in Europe or North America and built handsome palaces in Havana where they and their families lived sumptuously. Justo Cantero, a planter in Trinidad, built a house with a Roman bath with two heads of cherubs, one continuously spouting gin (for men) the other eau de cologne (for women).

An essential part of Cuban affairs was the great contribution that fortunes there made to enterprises in Spain. The financial connections are not easy to disentangle. But the relation was close. Juan Güell y Ferrer, for example, invested his Cuban money in Catalan cotton. Pablo de Espalza, another Cuban millionaire, founded the Banco de Bilbao of which he became first president. Manuel Calvo helped to finance the election of King Amadeo of Savoy in 1870. Lists of Cuban slave merchants include many who, like Juan Xifre, helped to finance the first stage of industrialization in Catalonia in the nineteenth century. Meantime captains-general, judges and other officials continued to rely on their stay in Cuba to make fortunes which they then transferred to Spain.

At the other end of the social scale were the slaves. The success of the nineteenth-century sugar economy and the rapid expansion of the slave trade to Cuba had meant that the relative balance between black and white in the island for a time vanished; in the first half of the century there had been a substantial black or mulatto majority. But by the 1860s whites, due to substantial immigration in the middle of the century, had become once more the largest ethnic group. Out of a population of about 1.4 million in 1869, some 27 per cent (360,000) were slaves (compared with 44 per cent in the 1840s). About a third of the slaves worked to a greater or lesser extent in the countryside. Most slaves in the 1860s had been introduced into the island illegally; their importers had contravened the anti-slave trade laws of 1820 and 1845 and had successfully avoided the British navy's anti-slave trade patrols operating under the Anglo-Spanish treaties of 1817 and 1835. Slaves could still purchase their freedom by the old system of *coartación*, or purchase of freedom in instalments; perhaps 2,000 did this every year in the 1850s. Many mothers could buy freedom for their babies for a modest sum. Otherwise a slave had to pay his own market price – $500 or so in the 1830s, $1,000 or so in 1860. In 1860 about 16 per cent (240,000) of the total population were believed to be freed blacks or mulattos, admitted without too many questions into the bureaucracy, or the university.

The immediate consequence of the collapse of annexations with the defeat of the South in the American Civil War was the formation of a pressure group among prominent Cuban planters to secure some at least of the constitutional reforms now being pursued in Spain itself by progressive merchants. Some of the planters concerned were, like Miguel Aldama, ex-annexationists. But they were mostly less rich than those who had favoured annexation – as is evident from the fact that few of those concerned in these schemes, at least in the 1860s, were men who possessed mills with the most advanced sugar technology. (Aldama was an exception.) They desired a reduction of the powers of the captain-general, a constitutional assembly, taxation accompanied by representation – and an extension of the powers of the municipal councils.

This generation of reform-minded planters had also become convinced that with the outbreak of the American Civil War the slave trade would soon be brought to a halt. In 1862 a United States slave captain, Captain Nathaniel Gordon, was hanged for carrying 890 slaves on his ship to Havana — the first such punishment ever for a United States citizen. In the same year the United States and Britain initiated combined operations for the final suppression of the Cuban slave trade. By the time the Spanish government itself introduced new legislation in 1866 the trade had already virtually ceased; the last known importation of slaves into Cuba took place in 1867. Many reformers in Spain and Cuba supported the abolition of the Cuban slave trade in the belief that slavery itself would be preserved in the island. But since the institution of slavery was dependent on the continued importation of slaves — as in Brazil the slave population was never able to reproduce itself naturally — it was realized that one day Cuba would have to face the future without slaves and that alternative sources of labour would have to be found. Some planters were already arguing on economic grounds that in any case contract labour was preferable to slave labour, not least because slave prices had more than doubled during the previous twenty years. Experimental contracts were made with Gallegos, Canary Islanders, Irishmen and Indians from Yucatán. Most satisfactory were the Chinese: some 130,000 were introduced between 1853 and 1872 in conditions even worse than those of the slave trade from Africa, if figures for mortality on the journey mean anything.

The Cuban reformers of the 1860s were on good terms with two enlightened captains-general — Francisco Serrano y Domínguez (1859–62) and Domingo Dulce y Garay (1862–6). It was agreed in 1865 that a Cuban commission should go to Madrid to discuss the island's political future. The next year elections were held for the first time in Cuba, with a high property qualification, it is true, but on the same basis as those which were held in Spain. The *Junta de Información* in Madrid, which also included Puerto Rican representatives, discussed every aspect of constitutional reform as well as the question of slavery. The Cuban members believed they had made some progress by persuading the Spanish government of the need for constitutional change, but all their work was undone by another *coup d'état* in Madrid, bringing the intolerant General Narváez to power. The reformers returned to Havana with no policy and no future to offer. Constitutional reform within the Spanish empire seemed as closed an avenue as annexation to the Union.

The Cuban reformers who had gone to Madrid were too gentlemanly to contemplate a rebellion for independence. Perhaps they were still affected by the memories of the Haiti rebellion of the 1790s. At all events they could not risk provoking a crisis in which they might lose their slaves immediately, however much they might contemplate the idea of a gradual extinguishing of slave society. This was even more the case with the very rich, the great moguls of nineteenth-century Cuba, who had never contemplated any political innovation other than annexation to the United States. The small number of early trade unionists, especially in the tobacco factories, were interested in higher wages, better working conditions and shorter hours. They had as yet no thoughts about the political future of Cuba save as a Spanish colony which sold both cigars and sugar on a large scale to the United States. The only section of the Cuban community interested in rebellion in the 1860s were the smaller sugar and coffee planters in the east of the island. Impoverished, preoccupied by great world events as only a parochial planter class can be, they had made little money out of recent sugar harvests, since they had resources neither for new machinery nor for new slaves. Their mills were too far from Havana – with no railways and no roads to get to them – to be able easily to command loans from Havana merchants. Some of the planters of the east anticipated the emancipation of slaves by letting them out for wages during the harvest. Some of the families had enough money, true, to send their children to Europe or the United States for education. These returned, however, with their heads full of a spirit of revolution, disturbed by colonial conventions and ashamed of colonial repression. It was among them, particularly among the freemasons, that the spirit of rebellion spread in 1867 and 1868.

Carlos Manuel de Céspedes was a typical small sugar planter of this type, though he was uncharacteristic in one respect: much of his youth had been spent in abortive political activity in Spain. In 1868, he held a public meeting at his farm in Oriente province at which he romantically adjured his hearers to take the road followed elsewhere in Latin America by Bolívar and San Martín. Doubtless little would have come of Céspedes's movement had it not coincided with a major upheaval in Spain: a military rebellion and the flight of Queen Isabel II from Madrid in September 1868. A rebellion in Puerto Rico followed. Then another east Cuban planter, Luis Figueredo, hanged a Spanish tax collector on his farm and invited denunciation as an outlaw. The Cuban rebellion began when Céspedes freed his slaves and founded a small army of 147 men at his estate at La Demajagua on October 10, issuing a declaration, the 'Grito de Yara', which echoed the American Declaration of Independence. This was the beginning of the Ten Years War (1868–78), Cuba's first war of independence.

By 1868 the pattern of future Cuban society had been established as it was to remain. The population of Cuba had assumed most of its modern characteristics – slightly over half Spanish in origin and slightly under half black or mulatto, with a small number of Chinese, Anglo-Saxons, French and others. The proportion has remained much the same since 1868, despite the final eclipse of slavery[3] and a substantial immigration from Spain in the first quarter of the twentieth century. Sugar was very definitely the dominant industry by the 1860s, producing substantial quantities for an ever more voracious world market. That too has remained the case. The whole Cuban economy already revolved, as it has done ever since, around the sugar harvest. There might soon be some changes in the organization of Cuban sugar, characterized by a drop in the number of sugar mills and an increase in the acreage planted with cane, which was occasioned by the availability of cheap steel for longer railway lines and also by the challenge of sugar beet in the 1870s. That, in turn, led to the eclipse of the old *criollo* aristocracy and its substitute after 1900 by companies – themselves substituted by state farms after 1960. But the place of sugar within the national economy has not much varied. Finally, two generations of romantic flirting with the idea of rebellion, in exile or in secret places in Havana, had given to the Cuban national culture an affection (if not an affectation) for heroism and revolt.

---

[3] During the Ten Years War the Spanish Cortes passed the Moret Law (1870), a qualified law of free birth which also freed slaves over 60. (And in 1873 slavery was abolished in Puerto Rico.) A law of 29 July 1880 abolished slavery in Cuba, but instead of indemnity to slave-owners a system of *patronato* (apprenticeship) was to continue until 1888. In the event, the *patronato* was abolished on 7 October 1886 (with only some 25,000 *patrocinados* in Cuba at the time). On the abolition of slavery in Cuba, see Raúl Cepero Bonilla, *Azúcar y abolición* (Havana, 1948); Arthur F. Corwin, *Spain and the abolition of slavery in Cuba, 1817–1886* (Austin, Texas, 1967); Franklin W. Knight, *Slave society in Cuba during the nineteenth century* (Madison, 1970); Rebecca J. Scott, 'Gradual abolition and the dynamics of slave emancipation in Cuba, 1868–86', *Hispanic American Historical Review*, 63/3 (1983), 449–77 and *Slave emancipation in Cuba: the transition to free labour* (forthcoming at the time). (Editor's note.)

2

CUBA, *c.* 1860 – *c.* 1930

In the 1860s, Cuba, the richest and most populated of Spain's two remaining American colonies, faced serious economic and political problems. The period of sustained growth, which beginning in the late eighteenth century had transformed the island into the world's foremost sugar producer, had begun to slow down during the previous decade. The production and export of sugar, the colony's staple product, continued to expand, but growing competition from European and American sugar beet and the development of new sugar-cane producing regions posed a threat to the future.

Since the 1840s, conscious of that threat, many alert hacendados (sugar-mill owners) began efforts to modernize (essentially to mechanize) the industry, while doubling their demands for reform of the archaic colonial commercial system. Spain economic weakness, and specifically her lack of sugar refineries and inability to absorb Cuba's sugar production, increasingly revealed Cuba's colonial dilemma: growing economic dependence on markets and technology which her mother country could not provide.

Furthermore, the future of slavery, for centuries an essential element in sugar production, had become bleak. The slave trade to Cuba had been declared illegal by treaties between Spain and Britain in 1817, but the trade managed to continue until 1835, when another treaty between the two nations and stricter vigilance on the part of the Spanish authorities forced it to decline yearly. By 1860 the infamous trade had virtually disappeared.[1] During the 1840s and 1850s, some hacendados had placed

[1] By then the number of slaves had declined from a peak of almost half a million (44 per cent of the population) in 1841, to 367,350 (under 30 per cent of a population of 1.4 million) in 1860. Ramón de la Sagra, *Cuba en 1860. Cuadro de sus adelantos en la población, la agricultura, el comercio y las rentas públicas* (Paris, 1863; first published as a Supplement to his twelve-volume *Historia política y natural de la Isla de Cuba*), 9.

their hopes for continued slavery on annexation by the United States, and had even helped to organize armed US expeditions to Cuba, but the victory of the North in the American civil war put an end to that particular brand of annexationist thought. After 1865, the hacendados were fighting a rearguard action, trying to delay abolition and to obtain guarantees of compensation for the loss of their slaves.

Thus by the mid 1860s the majority of the Cuban economic elite concentrated their efforts on obtaining the necessary reforms from Spain to assure them free trade, the *gradual* abolition of slavery with compensation for their losses, and increasing participation in the colonial government. Opposing them, the most intransigent *peninsulares* (Spaniards), who dominated trade and colonial administration, denounced every reform as a step towards independence. One of the arguments most frequently used by the *peninsulares* was that any rebellion against Spain would reproduce in Cuba the fate of Haiti, where in the 1790s a struggle among the whites ended with a devastating and successful rebellion by the blacks.

Convinced that Spain was unwilling or incapable of conceding any reform, a minority of Cubans did in fact favour independence. Some of them, influenced by a nationalistic sentiment seeded at the beginning of the century by philosophers like Félix Varela and poets like José María Heredia, envisaged a free sovereign Cuba, with close economic ties to the United States. Others wanted to end Spanish rule and then, as Texas had done in the 1840s, seek annexation by the United States, a nation which symbolized for them both economic progress and democracy.

During the previous decade opposition to Spain had not only substantially increased, but had spread to all sectors of the population. Burdened by high and unfair taxation (among other things, Cuba was forced to pay for or contribute towards the Spanish expedition to Mexico in 1862, her military campaigns in Africa, the naval war against Peru and Chile in 1866, as well as the salaries of the entire Spanish diplomatic corps in Latin America), governed arbitrarily by a growing swarm of Spanish bureaucrats, discriminated against by *peninsulares* who considered themselves superior to the native population, many Cubans, including the free blacks who constituted 16 per cent of the population, were beginning to express their resentment. The island was becoming divided into two hostile camps: Cubans versus Spaniards. Cubans outnumbered Spaniards 12 to 1 in the western and 23 to 1 in the eastern provinces.

In 1865, the reform movement gained momentum. Political change in

Spain brought the liberals to power and a Junta de Información, formed by members elected in Cuba, Puerto Rico and the Philippines, was to convene in Madrid to discuss constitutional reforms and the slavery question. The Junta, however, was abruptly dismissed in 1867 and its proposals were totally ignored by the Spanish government. In the meantime, an international economic crisis rocked Cuba, forcing a reduction of the *zafra* (sugar harvest). As a result, riding high on the crest of a general and bitter anti-Spanish feeling, the pro-Independence groups decided that their hour had come. 'A España no se le convence, se le vence!' (Spain should be defeated, not convinced!) became their defiant slogan.

In the western regions (the provinces of Pinar del Río, Havana, Matanzas and part of Las Villas), where 80 per cent of the population and 90 per cent of sugar wealth was concentrated, the majority of hacendados were reluctant to risk war with Spain and favoured reforms. In the eastern regions (the provinces of Oriente, Camagüey and the rest of Las Villas), however, with fewer sugar mills and slaves and a more vulnerable economy, hacendados such as Ignacio Agramonte, Francisco Vicente Aguilera, and Carlos Manuel de Céspedes believed in the possibility and necessity of defeating Spain. Moreover, as the construction of roads and railways had been determined by the needs of the sugar industry, the larger and less developed eastern region of the island lacked good communications, a factor which, by hindering the deployment of Spanish troops, emboldened pro-Independence groups. The town of Bayamo, in the rebellious department of Oriente, emerged as the centre of conspiracies. The majority of the clergy were Spaniards, and revolutionary leaders therefore were able to use the secrecy of masonic lodges to organize and co-ordinate their actions.[2]

Recent international developments also encouraged those willing to fight for independence. Spain's lack of success in the Dominican Republic, which she occupied in 1861 and abandoned in 1865, and the failure of Napoleon III in Mexico, resulting in the execution of Emperor Maximilian I, convinced many Cubans that the European powers, and especially declining Spain, could be defeated by determined national

---

[2] In contrast to what had occurred in the rest of Latin America, during the wars of independence in Cuba the clergy remained almost unanimously loyal to Spain. This was primarily due to the Spanish liberal reforms of 1826–41, which deprived the clergy of most of its resources, and to the Concordat of 1851, which practically transformed the church into an instrument of the Spanish state. After independence, the memory of this anti-Cuban attitude considerably weakened the influence of the Catholic church in Cuba.

resistance. The Dominican episode also had more direct consequences: many militarily experienced Dominicans who came to reside in the eastern part of Cuba were to make an invaluable contribution to the Cuban rebellion.

During the summer of 1868 the conspirators stepped up their activities; refusal to pay taxes spread, propaganda became more belligerent, and emissaries were sent to Havana in a futile effort to persuade reformists to join the rebellion. Contrary to the wishes of more impatient leaders such as Céspedes, the conspirators agreed in July that the rebellion should begin in December.

Several events precipitated the crisis. On 18 September, the growing instability of the Spanish monarchy led to a military rebellion in Spain which ended the rule of Isabel II. Cuban colonial authorities, weary of the results of such political upheaval, adopted a passive, observant attitude. A minor rebellion in the Puerto Rican town of Lares (22 September 1868) was easily crushed by the Spanish forces, but unfounded reports spread throughout Cuba that numerous Puerto Rican groups were ready to continue the struggle. Finally, there were rumours in Oriente that the Spanish authorities were informed of the conspiracy and prepared to take the necessary actions. Convinced that to wait would be disastrous, Céspedes decided to force the issue. On 10 October, without consulting other leaders and with a few followers, he raised the banner of rebellion at his plantation La Demajagua and proclaimed the independence of Cuba.

The colonial government was in no position to react decisively. Poorly informed of incidents in Oriente, and troubled by political turmoil in Spain, Captain General Lersundi paid little attention to news of the uprisings. Despite an initial defeat at the town of Yara, Céspedes had time to increase his heterogeneous band by enlisting discontented Cubans and Dominicans with combat experience. On 18 October he attacked and captured the town of Bayamo, temporarily silencing accusations of personal ambition and confirming himself as leader of the insurrection.

News of Bayamo's fall electrified the island and mobilized the Cuban population. In Oriente and Camagüey several groups followed Céspedes's example and rose in arms. Rebel bands appeared in the central provinces of Las Villas. Even young Havana reformists hastened to join the insurgents. Early in 1869 the colonial government, having dismissed the insurrection as a local incident, was confronted by a rapidly expanding rebellion. Cuba's first war of independence had begun.

Although confined to the eastern region of the island, the war lasted ten years and forced Spain to send over one hundred thousand troops to the 'ever faithful Cuba'. The rebels' courage and tenacity was aided by several basic factors. Peasant support and topographical knowledge gave them superior mobility. Often aware of Spanish troop movements, they could select the best zones for combat or concealment. They became experts in guerilla warfare with the Cuban climate their strongest ally. Unaccustomed to the tropics, many Spanish soldiers became sick with yellow fever and malaria. Fatigue and exhaustion repeatedly disrupted Spanish army operations.

Political conditions in Spain also aided the Cubans. During the war, Spain witnessed the abdication of Isabel II; a military regency; the reign of Amadeo of Savoy (1871–3); the proclamation of a Republic; the restoration of Alfonso XII; and a second Carlist War (1872–6). As a result, the Spanish army in Cuba seldom received adequate attention or supplies. Traditional bureaucratic corruption and political favouritism undermined any serious military effort. Symptomatically, during the first eight years of the war eleven officers held the rank of Captain General in Cuba.

The Cubans had their own share of problems. Divided by petty regionalism, class origins, and different concepts of military strategy, they lacked the discipline and unity essential for victory. In the town of Guaimaro, in Oriente, the Constituent Assembly of 1869 officially proclaimed the Republic, promulgated a liberal constitution, nominally abolished slavery, and approved a motion for annexation by the United States. Unfortunately, it also established a separation of power which was to hamper and ultimately doom the war effort. Authoritarian tendencies, such as those exhibited by Céspedes, frightened delegates under the influence of Camagüeyan leader Ignacio Agramonte, a romantic young lawyer, into creating a legalistic Republic where military commanders could not act without congressional approval. Uninterrupted friction between civil and military authorities followed this decision. Most rebel military leaders were eventually either removed or challenged by an itinerant government (Bayamo was eventually recaptured by the Spaniards) unwilling to yield yet incapable of imposing full authority.

By 1874 many of the elite who had initiated the war – Aguilera, Agramonte, Céspedes – were either dead or in exile. New leaders, humbler in origin but forged in battle, radicalized the struggle. The Dominican Máximo Gómez and the Cuban mulatto Antonio Maceo were foremost among them. The United States' strict neutrality and disregard of Cuban pleas for recognition[3] had by then dispelled all illusions of American support, practically erasing annexationist tendencies among the rebels.

The growing exhaustion of funds supplied by Cuban exiles and the end of Spain's Carlist War, which allowed Madrid to concentrate its efforts on Cuba, convinced Cuban military leaders that their only hope for victory was to invade the island's rich western provinces. The ruin of so many sugar mills would deprive Spain of vital revenues and leave thousands of slaves and peasants free to join the rebels. With a depleted treasury and a seemingly interminable war, Spain would be forced to accept Cuban independence. Early in 1875 Gómez defeated the Spanish forces in Las Villas and was prepared to carry out this plan when another internecine dispute disrupted the project. Returning to Oriente to restore order, he was instead forced to resign his command. The revolutionary momentum began to turn.

By combining military pressure with generous amnesty offers and promises of reform, General Martínez Campos, the new Captain General, further divided the already demoralized rebels. Late in 1877 Cuban President Tomás Estrada Palma was captured. In February 1878 a Cuban commission presented the Spanish government with armistice terms. With the approval of the Spanish authorities, the peace treaty under which the autonomy recently granted to Puerto Rico would be extended to Cuba was signed in the hamlet of Zanjón. (In fact Puerto Rican autonomy was rescinded later in the same year.) Demanding independence and the immediate abolition of slavery, General Antonio Maceo rejected the treaty at Baraguá, and announced his intention of continuing the war. It was a spectacular but a futile gesture: in May the last rebel forces accepted the Zanjón Treaty. Gómez, Maceo and many other Cuban leaders went into exile, and Cuba's first war for independence ended.

The entire conflict, known in Cuba as the Ten Years' War, contributed to the growth and maturity of a national conscience. The vague feeling of collective identity which had emerged in the early nineteenth century became a deep, ardent sentiment. Although racism remained, Spanish

---

[3] President Ulysses S. Grant was inclined to recognize Cuban belligerency, but his Secretary of State, Hamilton Fish, who maintained the traditional US policy of keeping Cuba under the control of a weak power like Spain until the conditions were ripe for annexation, always managed to thwart his intentions. See Philip S. Foner, *A history of Cuba and its relations with the United States* (2 vols., New York, 1962–3), II, 204–20.

warnings that an anti-colonial struggle would trigger off a racial war similar to that of Haiti now carried little weight since blacks had joined whites in the fight against Spain. Memories of Cuban heroes and Cuban victories – and of Spanish brutality (such as the execution of seven university students in 1871) – stirred patriotic emotions which made full reconciliation extremely difficult. On the Spanish side, the war increased the anti-Cuban animosity and distrust felt by the most intransigent *peninsulares*.

The vast destruction of hundreds of sugar mills in the east opened those provinces to expansionist forces in the new modernized sector of the sugar industry. Even in the undamaged western regions the war accelerated a similar process. Many important hacendados began building bigger, more efficient mills, while those who had suffered severe losses or could not afford larger mills were transformed into *colonos* (planters who sold their sugar to the mills), slowing down the trend towards *latifundismo* in the island. Ultimately, the war signalled the decline of the Cuban landed aristocracy, who were decimated and ruined by the long struggle or forced by the Spanish authorities to sell their lands and mills. In many cases American capitalists acquired both at very low prices, marking the beginning of American economic penetration into Cuba.

The three most important developments in the period between the Zanjón peace (1878) and the Second War of Independence which began in 1895 were the rise and decline of the Autonomist party; the United States' displacement of Spain as Cuba's economic metropolis; and the formation and growing influence of José Martí's Cuban Revolutionary party.

In Havana, a few months after the end of the Ten Years' War, prominent members of the old reformist group and many Cubans anxious for reconstruction and prosperity founded a liberal party, the Autonomist party. This powerful national organization's main objective was the achievement of Cuban autonomy by peaceful means. When in 1880 General Calixto García and other rebel leaders attempted an uprising, the party swiftly condemned their action and proclaimed its loyalty to Spain. Simultaneously opposed by pro-Independence groups and by the traditionally intransigent *peninsulares*, the *autonomistas* faced formidable obstacles. Nevertheless, hopes of reform and division among the war veterans gave the *autonomistas* the temporary support of many

Cubans. Despite their organization and brilliant political campaigns, however, their victories were marginal. Ten years after the Treaty of Zanjón, although Spain had finally abolished slavery (1880–6) and extended certain political rights to Cubans, inequality prevailed. In 1890, for example, much to the *autonomistas'* dismay Spain proclaimed universal suffrage, but excluded Cuba. Three years later the Spanish minister Antonio Maura, aware of mounting Cuban irritation, proposed new reforms leading to autonomy for the island. His proposals met with the usual resistance from conservatives in Spain and Havana, and with scepticism from most Cubans. When Maura resigned in 1894 the *autonomistas* had already lost the confidence of the majority and Martí's new Cuban Revolutionary party had succeeded in uniting most groups in favour of independence. A new economic crisis dashed the last hopes of the *autonomistas*. By 1894 a new war for independence loomed on the horizon.

The growing absorption of Cuban exports, notably sugar, by the American market can be demonstrated by a few figures. In 1850 Cuba exported produce worth 7 million pesos to Spain, and 28 million pesos to the USA. By 1860 the figures had risen to 21 million and 40 million pesos respectively. By 1890 Spain imported produce worth 7 million pesos and the United States 61 million pesos. This economic dependence made the island extremely vulnerable to any change in US trade policy. In 1894 when the American government passed the Wilson Tariff on sugar imports, the repercussions in Cuba were disastrous. Exports to the USA fell from 800,000 tons in 1895 to 225,231 tons in 1896. Thus the crisis in the sugar industry, already plagued by a decline in prices and growing international competition, became more acute in 1895, creating a favourable atmosphere for a new rebellion.

The opening of the Second War of Independence centred on José Martí, the man who forged the union of Cuban patriots and founded the Cuban Revolutionary party. Born in Havana on 28 January 1853 of Spanish parents, Martí was a gifted child. Devoted to reading and of a solitary nature he very early on developed a consuming love for Cuba. In 1870 a naive letter criticizing a colleague who enlisted in the Spanish army led the colonial authorities to sentence him to six years of hard labour. Deported to Spain, after a few months in prison he published his first book, *El presidio político en Cuba*, which expressed not only anger, but compassion for the oppressors. In the prologue he wrote what would become the motto of his life: 'Only love creates.' After completing his studies at the University of Zaragoza, Martí travelled throughout Europe, worked as a journalist in Mexico, and taught in Guatemala. He returned to Cuba in 1878 but was forced by the Spanish authorities to leave the island, and he moved to Venezuela. In 1881 he settled in New York where his reputation as a writer enabled him to survive on articles sent to several Latin American journals. Martí's unusually passionate prose and original poetic style increased his reputation in Latin American literary circles. Eventually he concentrated all his energies on the struggle for Cuban independence. His first task, the uniting of bickering Cuban exile groups, was made even more difficult by his lack of a military record. Travelling, lecturing and publishing, he overcame criticism and suspicion, rekindled Cuban enthusiasm, and established a basis for union. In 1892 he created the Cuban Revolutionary party. With his usual fervour, Martí mobilized all available resources for a 'just and necessary war'. His urgency was stimulated by an awareness of growing imperialist trends in the United States.

A man of deep democratic conviction, Martí appealed to Cubans of all races and classes to fight for an economically and politically independent Republic which would guarantee justice and equality not only to all Cubans but even to Spaniards who decided to stay in the island. Fearing that a long war would provoke the rise of military *caudillos*, the destruction of Cuban wealth, and intervention by the USA, Martí planned a struggle which differed from the Ten Years' War. A mass rebellion was to occur simultaneously in every region of the island with sufficient force to guarantee a quick victory. Supported by some rich Cubans and the majority of Cuban tobacco workers in Florida, Martí laboriously gathered as much money as he could and worked feverishly to assemble supplies for the initial blow. In January 1895 military equipment for three expeditions was gathered at the port of Fernandina in Florida. Suddenly, on 14 January, the American authorities confiscated the ships and their matériel.

This disaster drastically altered Martí's project and alerted the Spanish authorities to the magnitude of the conspiracy. To postpone the date for the insurrection would have endangered all those in Cuba committed to the rebellion. After a last desperate effort to obtain new supplies, Martí set the date for the rebellion and departed for the Dominican Republic in order to join Máximo Gómez.

According to plan, on 24 February small groups rose in arms in Oriente, Camagüey, Las Villas, Matanzas, and Havana. In the latter two (smaller) regions, where Spanish military power was concentrated, the rebellion was quickly subdued. Once more the eastern region of the island was to bear the brunt of the struggle. Maceo landed in Oriente on 1 April. On 15 April, after the proclamation in the Dominican Republic of the Manifesto of Montecristi expounding the causes of the war, Martí and Gómez embarked for Oriente. The following month Martí, who in defending the necessity of a civilian government capable of balancing the generals' power had clashed with General Maceo, was killed in a skirmish with the Spanish forces at Dos Ríos.

Martí's death deprived the rebellion of its most distinguished and respected civilian authority. Unrestrained by his presence, Generals Gómez and Maceo proceeded to organize a revolutionary government amenable to their ideas. Both recognized the need for a political organization which could obtain international acceptance and military assistance. But they had not forgotten the disruptive quarrels which had complicated the Ten Years' War. This time no civilian authority would interfere with their military plans. In September 1895, in the town of Jimaguayú, a hastily gathered constituent assembly approved a constitution, article IV of which stated, 'The Government Council shall intervene in the direction of military operations only when in its judgement it shall be absolutely necessary for the achievements of other political ends.'[4] Salvador Cisneros Betancourt, a rich and aristocratic Camagüeyan who had fought in the previous war, was selected as president, and Tomás Estrada Palma, the last president in arms in 1878, was confirmed as delegate and foreign representative of the Republic. Máximo Gómez was named commander-in-chief of the army and Antonio Maceo second in command. Both received sufficient authority to consider themselves almost independent of civilian restraint.

The convention of Jimaguayú symbolized other changes in the character of the war. Few of the delegates belonged to aristocratic families, slavery had disappeared as a divisive issue, annexation was not mentioned and the majority of the delegates were young and inexperienced men. As Enrique Collazo, a distinguished veteran of the Ten Years' War and future historian of this period, put it, 'this revolution was the revolution of the poor and the young'.[5] However, contrary to Martí's vision it was also a war of generals.

[4] Leonel Antonio de la Cuesta and Rolando Alum Linera (eds.), *Constituciones Cubanas* (New York, 1974), 127. [5] Enrique Collazo, *Cuba independiente* (Havana, 1912), 195.

With the revolutionary government legally established, Gómez and Maceo were free to carry out their plan for invading the western regions. Spain's basic strategy was similar to that of the Ten Years' War. Commanded once more by General Martínez Campos, who had defeated the Cubans in the last conflict, Spanish troops built a series of fortified lines (*trochas*) to protect each province and impede rebel movements. This tactic enabled the Cubans to take the offensive. On 22 October 1895, symbolically in Baraguá, Maceo began his march to the west. Gómez awaited him with a small force in Las Villas. A general order had been given to the troops 'to burn and destroy everything that could provide income to the enemy'. By early 1896, having traversed the island in a brilliant campaign, Cuban forces were fighting in the vicinity of Havana with some of Cuba's richest zones wasted behind them.

To confuse the Spaniards and expand their operations, the two generals separated their columns on reaching Havana. Gómez returned to Las Villas while Maceo went on to invade Pinar del Río, the last western province. The invasion was successful, but Spain was not defeated. Martínez Campos was replaced by a tougher general, Valeriano Weyler, who arrived with large reinforcements. In Madrid, the Spanish minister Cánovas del Castillo stated his government's decision: 'Spain will fight to the last man and the last peseta.' The war continued.

With Weyler the struggle reached a new level of intensity. Determined to pacify Cuba at all costs, he took the offensive and rounded up peasants in the military zones into protected camps. Lack of food supplies and inadequate organization transformed this harsh but sound military measure into an inhuman venture which infuriated the rebels and provoked international protests. After nine months of Weyler's war of extermination only two Cuban provinces had been pacified. In December 1896, however, Weyler achieved his most spectacular success. Antonio Maceo, popularly known as the 'Bronze Titan', was killed in a minor battle in Havana province.

Maceo's death, a severe blow for the Cubans, came at a time when a confrontation between General Gómez and the Cuban revolutionary government had reached a critical level. The government tried to assert some measure of authority by attempting to curb Gómez's personal power. The general's reaction bordered on insurrection. The death of the 'Bronze Titan' shook both opponents. His son's heroic death at Maceo's side added a tragic aura to Gómez's reputation. And the declaration by President Grover Cleveland that a civilian Cuban government was a

mere 'pretence' made clear the need to compromise.[6] The government
left Gómez's power intact, while the general publicly assured Americans
that the freely elected government 'in arms' was the supreme authority
for all Cuban rebels.[7]

Spanish hopes of victory soared with Maceo's death. Weyler
concentrated forty thousand troops in Las Villas, where Gómez had his
headquarters, and confidently announced that the province would be
pacified in a matter of weeks. With only four thousand men, Gómez
fought his best campaign. Eluding the enemy, harassing its columns,
attacking by surprise, the old general managed not only to survive but to
inflict heavy losses. By May 1897, the Spanish offensive had lost its
momentum. In the meantime, in Oriente, profiting from the Spanish
army's concentration on Gómez, General Calixto García attacked and
captured the towns of Jiguani and Victoria de las Tunas, the latter a
strategic crossroads. Two months later Weyler was ordered back to
Spain. Cuban successes, the assassination in Spain of Weyler's protector,
minister Cánovas del Castillo (by an Italian anarchist who had been in
contact with Puerto Rican and Cuban exiles in Europe), and growing
American concern about the Cuban situation convinced Madrid that it
was time to attempt appeasement. The new moderate minister Praxedes
Sagasta promoted General Ramón Blanco to Captain General and sent
him to Cuba. Upon reaching Havana, General Blanco proclaimed Cuba's
autonomy and named several *autonomistas* as members of the new
government.

The Cuban situation had by this time become a major issue in the
United States. Convinced that American interests on the island were best
protected by Spain, which paid indemnities for damage done to
American-owned properties in Cuba, while disdaining the 'Cuban
rascals', President Cleveland maintained a 'neutrality' which essentially
favoured Spain. However, Congress and particularly the press inveighed
against Spanish policies and demanded Cuban recognition. With
President William McKinley's inauguration, the anti-Spanish campaign reached emotional proportions. Cubans became innocent victims
murdered by butchers like Weyler. At the same time sober, powerful
elements added their weight to the campaign. Imbued with Alfred

---

6 For Cleveland's declaration, followed by one even more explicit by Secretary of State Richard B.
   Olney, see *Foreign relations of the United States* (Washington, DC, 1897), xxix–xxx.
7 The compromise was actually a victory for General Gómez. For the text of Gómez's declaration,
   see Bernabe Boza, *Mi diario de guerra* (Havana, 1906), II, 14–17.

Mahan's ideas of sea power, expansionists such as Theodore Roosevelt welcomed the sight of the American flag in the Caribbean. And some American businessmen, no longer convinced of Spain's capacity to protect their interests in Cuba, increasingly favoured United States intervention.

Under the circumstances, President McKinley displayed remarkable restraint. In his annual message to Congress on 6 December 1897, he refused to recognize Cuban belligerency or independence, and proposed to await the outcome of the newly proclaimed autonomy. The waiting period was brief. The rebels refused to recognize the legitimacy of the new regime, and early in 1898 pro-Spanish elements in Havana launched violent demonstrations against General Blanco and Cuban autonomy. Unduly alarmed, the American consul, Fitzhugh Lee, asked the captain of the battleship *Maine*, on alert in Key West since December, to prepare to sail for Havana. On 24 January, the American government received permission to send the vessel on a 'friendly' visit to Cuba. The following day a silent crowd in Havana harbour witnessed the arrival of the *Maine*. Captain Sigsbee had waited until midday to give the Spaniards ample opportunity to gaze at the symbol of American naval power.

While the *Maine*'s extended visit annoyed the Spanish authorities, a diplomatic incident further strained the situation. A derogatory, private letter written by the Spanish Minister in Washington about President McKinley and Cuban *autonomistas* was intercepted by Cuban revolutionaries and released to the press. Neither the minister's resignation nor Spanish apologies helped to quell the excitement. The press focused on Spanish insincerity toward Cuban reforms and hostility to the United States. The agitation had not yet abated when on 15 February the *Maine* exploded, 260 members of the crew were killed. The Spanish authorities spared no effort to help the survivors and determined that an internal accident had caused the disaster. The United States appointed its own board of enquiry to investigate the issue. But those interested in war found a vindication and a popular slogan, 'Remember the *Maine*, "the hell with Spain".' On 25 February, acting on his own initiative, Assistant Secretary of State Theodore Roosevelt issued orders placing the navy on full alert.

As the possibilities of war increased, Cuba's future became a debated issue. American opinions ranged from assistance towards full independence to annexation. Open contempt for an inferior race permeated many American views. The US government's position, however,

remained unchanged: under no circumstances should a rebel government be recognized. On 9 April, yielding again to American pressure, the
Spanish government offered the rebels an unconditional, immediate
truce; the offer was rejected. Spain could do no more to avoid war. On 11
April, President McKinley sent Congress a message in which 'in the
name of humanity, in the name of civilization, and on behalf of
endangered American interests', he asked for powers to intervene
forcibly in Cuba. Five days later, after heated debates, Congress
approved a Joint Resolution the first article of which declared that 'the
Cuban people are, and of right ought to be, free and independent', and
the last stated that 'the United States hereby disclaims any disposition or
intention to exercise sovereignty, jurisdiction, or control over said island
. . . and asserts its determination . . . to leave the government and
control of the island to its people'. Four days later the war began. The
existence of a Cuban rebel government was totally ignored.

Inadequately informed about the intricacies of Washington politics,
Cuban rebels generally welcomed the entry of the United States into the
war. Martí, who had dreaded the possibility, and Maceo, who opposed it,
were dead. And after three years of bitter fighting the insurgents were
ready to co-operate with an ally who had promised independence and
guaranteed victory. General Calixto García, who in 1897 had written
'Americans have no reason for interfering in our political affairs, and, on
the other hand, we are not fighting to become a yankee factory',[8] was
convinced that the United States would respect Cuban sovereignty; and
Máximo Gómez, rejecting the Spanish General Blanco's last minute
appeal to join forces against 'the common enemy of our race', had
answered, 'I only know one race, humanity . . . up till now I have only
had cause to admire the United States . . . I do not see the danger of our
extermination by the USA to which you refer . . . If that happens, history
will judge them . . . it is too late for an understanding between your army
and mine.'[9]

The outbreak of war provoked a wave of national enthusiasm in the
United States and, surprisingly, in Spain too, where the public had been
deceived about the real strength of the United States navy and the
deplorable condition of its own. Since 1880, the United States had based

[8] García to Estrada Palma, 31 August 1897, in *Boletín del Archivo Nacional* (Cuba), 26 (January–
December 1936), 108–12.
[9] For the full text of the letter, see Amalia Rodríguez Rodríguez, *Algunos documentos políticos de
Máximo Gómez* (Havana, 1962), 12–13.

its military strategy on the concept that the country was 'a continental island', geographically shielded from any foreign attack. Accordingly, the navy, 'the aggressive arm of the nation', had received full attention, while the army barely subsisted. As late as 1897, General Schoefield asserted that the army should limit itself 'to act in support of naval operations'. American initial strategy was therefore based on the navy. By defeating the Spanish navy, blockading the island, and supplying the rebels, the USA would force the Spanish army in Cuba to surrender.

Following the policy determined by Washington, the US armed forces were to take no action that could be interpreted as recognition of any Cuban political authority. Rebel forces should be aided and used, but only on a limited scale and strictly for military purposes. The instructions received by Major William R. Schafter before landing his troops in Oriente were typical: 'You can call to your assistance any of the insurgent forces in that vicinity, and make use of such of them as you think are available to assist you, especially as scouts, guides, etc. . . . you are cautioned against putting too much confidence on any persons outside your troops.'[10]

In May, while Washington was beginning to carry out the initial military plan, mobilizing the navy and sending supplies to some Cuban rebels, the Spanish naval squadron under Admiral Cervera managed to enter Santiago de Cuba. Immediately blockaded by Admiral Sampson's fleet, the presence of the squadron nevertheless altered the planned US operations. The landing of troops to attack Santiago de Cuba became necessary. At first, lack of logistic preparation and fear of yellow fever[11] led to the preparation of a 'reconnaissance force' only. But by the end of May, the US government decided to send an expeditionary force capable of defeating the Spanish army in Santiago. That decision reduced the strategic importance of Cuban forces fighting in other areas of the island. Only the army of General Calixto García, which controlled most of Oriente, was considered valuable. Consequently contacts with other Cuban leaders, including commander-in-chief Máximo Gómez, were practically suspended.[12]

[10] R. A. Alger [US Secretary of War], *The Spanish-American War* (New York, 1901), 64.

[11] The Americans knew, through impressive figures, the devastation caused in the Spanish army by yellow fever. According to Manuel Muñoz de Lara, *La España del siglo XIX* (Barcelona, 1975), 92, by May 1897 the Spanish army had had 2,129 dead in combat, 8,627 injured, and 53,000 dead or critically ill because of yellow fever. See also Pedro Roig, *La guerra de Martí* (Miami, 1984), 65–6.

[12] It was not until July that General Gómez received a supply expedition from the USA. The condition of the Cuban troops after three years of fighting can be measured by the fact that many soldiers became ill, and some of them died, after devouring American food rations.

Washington's policy of non-recognition was eased by the political weakness of the Cuban revolutionary government. Since the beginning of the war, rebel generals had frustrated all attempts to increase the government's authority. Consequently, the civilian branch of the 'Republic in arms', which Martí had so vigorously defended, had been reduced to a voice without much power. Even at this crucial moment, when the government was desperately struggling to gain official US recognition, the generals failed to support it. Máximo Gómez believed that President McKinley was withholding diplomatic recognition until a true Cuban government was established: 'this government', he wrote, 'is not the result of an Assembly but of the army'.[13] And when, ignoring the Cuban rebel government, American forces established direct relations with General Calixto García, the general acted as if his own government did not exist.

The American expeditionary force attacking Santiago received full support from García's forces. Besides providing scouts and fighting at its side, they kept Spanish garrisons immobilized in the rest of the provinces. By July, despite heroic Spanish resistance, the situation in the city was desperate. Dismissing Admiral Cervera's arguments, Captain General Blanco ordered the fleet to break the blockade. On 3 July 1898, the entire Spanish squadron was annihilated by the overwhelmingly superior American fleet. A few days later, Santiago was occupied by American forces who forbade Cuban rebels to enter the city. Defeated in Manila as well as Santiago, and with Puerto Rico already under American control, Spain sued for peace. While the terms were being discussed in Paris, American troops began to occupy Cuba. On 10 December, with no Cuban representatives, a peace treaty was signed ending Spanish domination of Cuba, Puerto Rico and the Philippines.

The American Military Government in Cuba (1899–1902) faced grave and urgent problems. After three years of war the island was devastated. Population had declined from 1,850,000 in 1894 to 1,689,600 in 1898. Hunger and disease were rampant, and the economy bordered on collapse. Four-fifths of the sugar estates were in ruins; the 1898 *zafra*

---

13 Gómez to Brigadier Méndez Capote in Amalia Rodríguez Rodríguez, *Documentos políticos*, 31. In a strict sense, the general, who knew well how the constituent assembly at Jimaguayú had been formed, was right. But he failed to realize how important it was at this juncture to have a civilian government, backed by the Cuban army, capable of dealing with the USA.

was about two-thirds less than in 1895. About 90 per cent of the island's cattle had been lost, and the tobacco industry had virtually ceased to exist. Communications had broken down. Scattered, poorly equipped, and hungry, the Cuban rebel army nevertheless kept a weary eye on the actions of the American authorities. The possibility of an armed confrontation between former 'allies' became a source of concern for Washington.

The Military Government reacted with efficient energy. Within two years the Cuban army had been peacefully disbanded, public health improved (a cure for yellow fever was finally discovered by Dr Carlos J. Finlay, a Cuban, and Dr Walter Reed) and communications expanded. A new educational system began to emerge. Simultaneously economic recovery began. With less land and capital requirements than sugar, the tobacco industry recuperated rapidly. Held back by low international prices and discriminatory American tariff barriers (sugar imports from Puerto Rico and the Philippines were exempt), Cuba's sugar production rose more slowly. In 1902, despite an influx of American and British capital, the total sugar crop value was $34,850,618, well below the level of 1894.

Favoured by US control over the island – and the weakening of local capital – American capital expanded its penetration in the sugar industry, and began to control railways, public utilities, tobacco and minerals. The immediate result of such growing dominance was the formulation of a powerful Washington lobby seeking better commercial relations with Cuba. As early as 1902, President Roosevelt recommended a reciprocity treaty with Cuba, stating that 'it is eminently for our own interests to control the Cuban market'.

Following the war Cuba's political future seemed clouded. Victory in the 'splendid little war' had encouraged American expansionist tendencies which saw no difference between Cuba, Puerto Rico and the Philippines. Consequently according to many American newspapers Cubans were no longer heroic independence fighters but had become a racially heterogeneous bunch of illiterates unfit to govern themselves. The Teller Amendment (Article 4 of the Joint Resolution) had, however, officially disclaimed any permanent interest in United States occupation and many politicians balked at the idea of openly breaking the agreement. Their uneasiness increased in 1899 when Filipino leader Emilio Aguinaldo, a hero of the fight against Spain, rebelled against

American forces. 'The thought of another Manila at Havana', wrote the Harvard historian Henry Adams, 'sobers even an army contractor.'[14] Cuban nationalism also proved too strong to be easily dismissed. The Cuban army had been disbanded for the minimal cost of three million American dollars, a sum proposed by General García and accepted by General Gómez, but mistrust of American intentions persisted. García died in 1899. Máximo Gómez, the most popular symbol of the Cuban Revolution, refused to go to Havana for the raising of the American flag on Morro's Castle. 'Ours', he wrote, 'is the Cuban flag, the one for which so many tears and blood have been shed . . . we must keep united in order to bring to an end this unjustified military occupation.'[15] The following year municipal elections were held in Cuba. Much to the disappointment of the Americans, nationalistic candidates won almost everywhere. Immediately following the elections, General Alejandro Rodríguez sent a telegram to President McKinley: 'The Cuban National Party, victorious in the election, salutes the worthy representative of the North American nation, and confidently awaits an early execution of the Joint Resolution.'[16]

In the United States anti-imperialist groups joined Democrats in attacking the 'colonialist' policies of the McKinley administration. In May 1900 large-scale embezzlements in the Havana post office were exposed, offering several Democratic senators an opportunity to demand American withdrawal. Under this pressure and with the presidential elections approaching, McKinley decided to establish a government in Cuba. A friendly dependent government seemed preferable to a battle over annexation. On 25 July 1900, General Leonard Wood, the American Military Governor, published a civil order for the provision of elections of delegates to a Cuban constitutional convention.

According to the electoral law established by the American authorities, the right to vote was restricted to males over 21 years of age who had become Cuban citizens under the terms of the peace treaty, and who fulfilled at least one of three alternative requirements: ability to read and write, ownership of property worth US$250 in American gold, or service in the Cuban rebel army. These restrictions, which disfranchised large sectors of the population, did not diminish enthusiasm for an election which heralded Independence. On 5 November 1900, in the Teatro

[14] Quoted in David F. Healy, *The United States in Cuba, 1898–1902* (Madison, 1963), 72.
[15] Fernando Freire de Andrade, 18 January 1899, in Amalia Rodríguez Rodríguez, *Documentos políticos*, 48.   [16] Quoted in Healy, *United States in Cuba*, 143.

Martí in Havana, 31 delegates representing six Cuban provinces met to begin the sessions of the Cuban Constitutional Convention. It was the delegates' duty, according to Wood's inaugural address, first to frame a constitution and then to formulate the relations which in their opinion 'ought to exist between Cuba and the United States'.

At the end of January 1901, after the completion of a constitution based on the American model, the delegates began working on the delicate subject of Cuban–American relations. Then General Wood confronted the convention with specific American demands. Among these were the right of the USA to intervene in Cuba and to establish a naval base in Guantánamo. Appalled and incensed, the delegates offered several counter-proposals aimed at saving Cuba's sovereignty. The issue was passionately debated in Cuba. Meanwhile, however, the US Congress approved a resolution introduced by senator Orville H. Platt (henceforth known as the Platt Amendment) which embodied American aspirations and was to be added to the Cuban constitution. The terms of the Amendment, especially Article 3 which gave the United States the right to intervene for 'the maintenance of a government adequate for the protection of life, property and individual liberties', provoked a wave of protests on the island. A delegation sent to Washington received assurances from Secretary of State Elihu Root that 'intervention was not synonymous with intermeddling, or interference with Cuban affairs',[17] but failed to modify American demands. As Manuel Sanguily, one of the most distinguished Cuban orators and patriots, expressed it, the Cuban dilemma was clear: a protected Republic or no Republic at all. On 28 May 1901, by a vote of fifteen to fourteen, the Convention adopted the proposed appendix to the constitution.

Once the constitution was promulgated it was necessary to proceed with presidential elections. When Máximo Gómez, the revered leader of Independence, refused the nomination, two other candidates emerged: General Bartolomé Masó, a prestigious military leader of limited talent, and Tomás Estrada Palma, who had been president of the 'Republic in arms' in the Ten Years' War, and had replaced Martí as the head of the Cuban Revolutionary Junta in exile. The former was the most popular; the latter, having spent most of his life in the United States, was basically unknown in Cuba, but he had the decisive support of Máximo Gómez

---

[17] Elihu Root repeated to the Cubans the official declaration he had sent to General Leonard Wood, Military Governor of Cuba. Root to Wood, 2 April 1901, Elihu Root Papers, Library of Congress, Washington, DC.

(who during the war had had many frictions with Masó), and the backing of General Wood. When Wood appointed five supporters of Estrada Palma to the electoral commission, General Masó withdrew from the race in protest. On 20 May 1902, amid popular jubilation, the duly elected Tomás Estrada Palma was inaugurated as Cuba's first president. That very day American troops began to evacuate the island. Witnessing the raising of the Cuban flag on Havana's Morro Castle, old Máximo Gómez expressed the emotions of many Cubans. 'At last, we have arrived!'

Economic recovery and honesty in public affairs characterized Estrada Palma's term in office (1902–6). A reciprocity treaty signed with the United States in 1903 gave Cuban sugar preferential treatment in the American market, reduced duties on American imports, and encouraged further American investment in the island, thus tying even more tightly Cuba's economy to the US market. Sugar production rose from 283,651 tons in 1900 to 1,183,347 in 1905, while cattle raising, the tobacco industry and several other sectors of the economy continued to recover rapidly from the devastation of the war.

The political situation, however, was less encouraging. Lacking any tradition of self-government or political discipline, with a low level of public education, and impoverished by the war, the Cubans found themselves trapped between growing American control of land and sugar, and Spanish domination of commerce, virtually guaranteed by the peace treaty between the USA and Spain. Politics thus became the principal avenue to economic improvement and one access to national resources. Consequently, political parties quickly became what González Lanuza, a distinguished university professor, called 'co-operatives organized for bureaucratic consumption'. Long-range programmes and loyalty to principles were sacrificed to immediate political gains. The growing, permanent shadow of American dominance and the presence of a numerous and increasing Spanish population (until 1934, thousands of Spanish immigrants poured annually into Cuba), who usually maintained a disdainful attitude toward Cuba's nationalism, were further obstacles to the development of a responsible and mature political system in the island. Old colonial vices, political corruption, local *caudillismo* and disregard for the law reappeared quickly. The manner in which the veterans of the War for Independence 'received' their compensation was distressingly symptomatic. Instead of distributing land, as suggested by some patriotic leaders, Sanguily among them, Congress decided to pay in cash. A foreign loan was obtained, but due to unscrupulous manipulations many soldiers received ridiculously small sums while a few politicians became rich.

Alarmed by these trends, Estrada Palma, an honest, stubborn and reserved man, decided to follow the advice of some of his aides and seek re-election. Apparently Washington favoured his decision,[18] but the president had misjudged the situation. He not only lacked popular sympathy, but he had also alienated many of his initial supporters, including Máximo Gómez, who died in 1905 full of misgivings about the future of the Republic. Estrada Palma's decision moved his two principal opponents, General José Miguel Gómez and Alfredo Zayas, to join forces to form a powerful Liberal party with the two leaders as candidates for president and vice president. Determined to win at any cost, the Moderate party leaders who supported Estrada Palma relied on the government's resources and forces to break the opposition. A series of violent confrontations culminating in the killing of Enrique Villuendas, a popular Liberal figure, persuaded the Liberals to abstain from the presidential campaign. Running alone, Estrada Palma, who probably did not know the extent of the fraud, was re-elected.

After this 'victory', the government did not attempt conciliation. Liberals continued to be harassed and excluded from bureaucratic positions. By the summer of 1906, the opposition was openly preparing for armed insurrection. Since the Republic had no army, the government faced the crisis with a Rural Guard thinly deployed in the interior of the island. When the rebellion broke in August, Estrada Palma, who had complete confidence in the backing of the United States, saw no other alternative than to ask Washington to intervene on his behalf. Deeply involved in the Panama Canal affair, President Theodore Roosevelt, however, wished to avoid any further action which could be interpreted as imperialistic. In an effort to avert intervention he sent two emissaries to Havana to seek a compromise between government and opposition. Regarding such impartiality as a vote of censure on his government, Estrada Palma resigned and made his entire cabinet resign too, leaving the Republic without a government and forcing the United States to take control of the island. Roosevelt immediately proclaimed that the USA had been compelled to intervene in Cuba and that their only purpose was

[18] See the favourable report (21 January 1905) of Squiers, US Minister in Havana, in Herminio Portell Vila, *Historia de Cuba en sus relaciones con los Estados Unidos y España* (4 vols., Havana, 1939), IV, 423.

to create the necessary conditions for a peaceful election. 'Our business,' he wrote, 'is to establish peace and order . . . start the new government and then leave the island.'[19]

The man selected to carry on this limited programme was Charles E. Magoon, a lawyer who had been a former governor of the Canal Zone and Minister to Panama. Hard working, conciliatory and 'without a touch of brilliance', Magoon failed to impress the Cubans, but as provisional governor achieved an adequate measure of success. The governor found that the main obstacle to rapid pacification was a group of businessmen, Cuban and foreign, who wanted to perpetuate the occupation by promoting unrest and spreading rumours about anti-American conspiracies. Unimpressed by their threats, Magoon reported that the majority of Cubans wanted to put an end to the intervention. Aware of the need for deeper economic and social reforms, but restrained by his instructions, Magoon inaugurated a programme of public works and attempted to appease bickering political groups by offering jobs and bureaucratic positions (a lesson not lost on the Cubans). He also encouraged the formation of a Conservative party to replace the discredited Moderates and modified the electoral laws to guarantee honest elections. The political reorganization was hindered by the reluctance of the property-owning class to participate in politics, an attitude the governor found irritating and irresponsible. Following Roosevelt's instructions, Magoon also set about organizing a small professional army capable of crushing any insurrection. Arguing that a professional army would soon become an instrument of repression against legitimate opposition, many Cubans – and several American advisers – counselled against the creation of a Cuban army, but it was officially formed in April 1908.

On 1 August 1908, with order fully re-established, municipal and provincial elections were held in which the Conservatives gained a surprising victory over a divided Liberal party. Realizing that defeat was inevitable in the forthcoming presidential elections if they remained disunited, the Liberal leaders José Miguel Gómez and Alfredo Zayas joined together once more on the same presidential ticket as they had in 1905. The Conservatives nominated General Mario G. Menocal and Rafael Montoro, a famous ex-*autonomista* orator. In November, after an orderly campaign tinged with anti-Americanism, the Liberals won

---

[19] Quoted in Allan Reed Millet, *The politics of intervention: the military occupation of Cuba, 1906–1909* (Columbus, Ohio, 1968), 146.

easily. A minor party formed by blacks, the Independent Party of Colour, which became significant later, failed to make any headway. On 28 January 1909, the birthday of José Martí, Magoon officially transferred power to President José Miguel Gómez. American troops stayed a little longer to ensure a peaceful transition, but on 31 March they withdrew from the island. With excessive optimism President Gómez declared, 'Once more Cubans have in their hands the destiny of their nation.'

The second American intervention (1906–9), in spite of its briefness, had a profound impact on Cuban life. Brought about by themselves, it seemed to justify Cuban doubts about their capacity for self-government. It undermined Cuban nationalism and reinforced the 'Plattist mentality' of relinquishing final political decisions to Washington. The submissive attitude of many powerful economic groups, which had annoyed Magoon, increased the gap between the elite who controlled the Cuban economy and the masses. The decline of nationalism and the growth of political cynicism alarmed many Cuban intellectuals who, like Enrique José Varona and Manuel Sanguily, tried to keep alive Martí's ideals.

José Miguel Gómez inherited a Republic with a little more than two million inhabitants (70 per cent white), quite a prosperous economy, and a public debt of $12 million left by Magoon's administration. A congenial, popular man, the president showed respect for democratic institutions, opposed direct American intervention in national affairs and demonstrated, by becoming rich and allowing others to follow his example, how politics could become highly profitable. Nicknamed 'the Shark', he inaugurated an era of public corruption. During his terms cockfighting and the national lottery, previously condemned as 'colonial vices', were re-established, the lottery evolving into an efficient machine of political debasement.

Two issues jeopardized the peace and sovereignty of the Republic in this period. One, the so-called 'Veterans question', was prompted by the permanence of Spanish or pro-Spanish elements in public positions which the veterans of the war for independence considered rightfully belonged to them. The agitation to expel these 'enemies' of Cuba became so threatening that American Secretary of State Philander Knox warned Gómez of the 'grave concern' of the United States. Opposition from many Cuban groups, fear of another American intervention, and some government concessions contributed to calm the veterans. The second issue proved more dangerous. The Independent Party of Colour, founded in 1907 by black extremists who, with valid arguments, accused

the Republic of betraying the black population, found its political
development blocked by the Morúa Law prepared in 1909 by the
Senate's president, Martín Morúa Delgado, a moderate black leader,
which banned political parties based on race or religion. Through secret
societies of African origin like the Nanigos and in open campaigns, the
independentistas fought for the abrogation of the law. In May 1912,
exasperated by their failure and perhaps encouraged by President
Gómez, who could have used a minor crisis as a step towards re-election,
the *independentistas* rebelled. Poorly organized and mainly confined to
Oriente province, the uprising, nevertheless, provoked a wave of panic
in the island. Equally alarmed, the United States government landed
Marines in Daiquiri and announced further actions if the Cuban
government failed 'to protect the lives or properties of American
citizens'. Protesting against such intervention, President Gómez ordered
the army to crush the rebellion. By June the leaders of the insurrection
were dead and their followers killed or disbanded. The fear and
resentment left by the episode hindered black participation in Cuban
politics for many years.

With presidential elections approaching, Gómez announced he would
not seek re-election. The Conservatives selected General Mario G.
Menocal as their candidate once again, with Enrique José Varona,
probably the most respected Cuban intellectual of the time, as his
running mate. Symptomatically, the slogan for the campaign was
'Honesty, Peace and Work'. Alfredo Zayas became the candidate of a
supposedly united Liberal party. But before the elections, the old
antagonism between Miguelistas (supporters of President Gómez) and
Zayistas surfaced again, splitting the party into two irreconcilable
factions. The subsequent alliance of the Miguelistas with the
Conservatives doomed Zayas's efforts, and Menocal won five of the six
provinces. On 20 May 1913, Gómez stepped down and a Conservative
president was sworn in. 'This orderly transmission of authority',
President Woodrow Wilson wrote to Menocal, 'is most gratifying and
seems to indicate that the Cuban people have successfully undergone one
of the severest tests of republican government.'[20]

The new president, a graduate in engineering from Cornell University, had been a distinguished military leader and a successful administrator of Chaparra, the largest sugar mill in Cuba, owned by the powerful

[20] United States Department of State, *Foreign relations of the United States, 1913* (Washington, DC, 1920), 337.

Cuban–American Sugar Company, with whom Menocal had a long and profitable association. Aristocratic and reserved, Menocal affected disdain for politics and displayed a paternalistic conservatism toward 'the working rabble'. He was to serve for two terms.

In his first term (1913–17), he partially fulfilled his electoral promises: official corruption was somehow restrained and, in spite of traditional congressional factionalism, some badly needed legislation was enacted. The Ley de Defensa Económica, which unified the armed forces, regulated the exportation of tobacco and created a Cuban currency, and the Ley de Accidentes del Trabajo (workmen's compensation) are two relevant examples. In 1915 the first labour congress was held in Havana; it demonstrated the emerging strength of the working class, the prevalent influence of anarchism, which had first penetrated the island in the nineteenth century through tobacco workers' organizations, and the tremendous difficulties involved in organizing nationally the sugar workers who constituted, as one of the speakers defined them, a 'rural proletariat'.

With improving economic conditions due to the first world war, and his popularity rising Menocal decided to seek re-election. As usual, the announcement triggered a hostile national reaction. The Liberals formed a united front behind the candidacy of Alfredo Zayas and Colonel Carlos Mendieta. By the summer of 1916 political tension was so charged with violence that a concerned President Wilson issued a warning that 'law and order should be maintained in Cuba at all costs'. Nevertheless increasing possibilities of war with Germany made Washington eager to avoid a crisis in Cuba. Consequently, Menocal, the representative of law and order, received full American support.

On 1 November 1916, noisy but on the whole peaceful elections were held. First reports showed Zayas winning by a large margin, but with the government controlling the information bulletins the number of pro-Menocal votes began to increase. Liberal protests were so intense that an open conflict was averted only when both parties agreed to allow the Supreme Court to decide the issue. After a brief deliberation the Supreme Court declared the Liberals victorious in the provinces of Camagüey and Havana, and the Conservatives in the provinces of Pinar del Río and Matanzas. New elections were to be held in Oriente, where both parties had equal strength, and Las Villas, a traditional Liberal stronghold.

Zayas's chances for electoral victory were thus reasonably high. But the Liberals decided not to wait for new elections. In February 1917, under the leadership of ex-president José Miguel Gómez and accusing the government of persistent repression, Liberals rebelled in several provinces; they rapidly captured Santiago de Cuba, Camagüey and several important towns in the interior. The pattern of 1906 – a rebellion spreading victoriously from the provinces towards Havana – seemed to be repeating itself. Unlike Estrada Palma, however, Menocal was an able military leader, had an army under his command and could count on assistance from the United States. Halted by stiff military resistance in Las Villas, the rebels were further disheartened by the publication of some diplomatic notes from the State Department to William Gonzalez, the American Minister in Cuba, stressing US support for 'legally established governments only'. The notes were accompanied by some display of American military forces at Santiago de Cuba and Guantánamo. The tide turned against the opposition. On 7 March 1917, surrounded by the army, José Miguel Gómez had to surrender in Las Villas. By May the rebellion was finished. For many Cubans, 'las notas de Mr Gonzalez (sic)' became a powerful symbol of American control over their internal political affairs. Menocal promptly paid his debt to Washington by declaring war on Germany immediately after the USA did.

Menocal's second term (1917–21), which began under these inauspicious circumstances, fell well below the level of his first. Corruption became rampant, fraudulent practices occurred in every election, and in spite of economic prosperity the president's popularity consistently declined. To make matters worse during Menocal's last year in power, sugar prices suddenly collapsed, plunging Cuba into her worst economic crisis and adding a new, dramatic dimension to the presidential campaign of 1920. Alfredo Zayas was the candidate of the Partido Popular Cubano, a small ex-Liberal faction, while José Miguel Gómez ran as the Liberal candidate. Zayas's possibilities of victory were quite remote until Menocal decided to back him with all the resources of power. During the elections violence and fraud were so scandalous that another Liberal uprising seemed imminent. Again the USA intervened. On 31 December, President Wilson ordered General Enoch Crowder, who had previous experience in Cuban affairs, to go to Havana as his personal representative. The Cuban government had not been consulted, and Menocal protested over such unilateral action, only to receive the answer that 'it has not been customary nor is it considered necessary for the President of the United States to obtain the prior consent of the President of Cuba to send a special representative to confer with him'.[21] On 6 January 1921, on board the battleship *Minnesota*, Crowder entered Havana.

Before dealing with the economic crisis, Crowder tried to solve the political crisis. Verifying the extent of the electoral fraud, he established new regulations to avoid its repetition and set 15 March as the date for new elections. A few days before that date, claiming lack of guarantees for free and fair elections, the Liberals decided to abstain. Running unopposed Alfredo Zayas was elected president. On 20 May amidst popular discontent and terrible economic conditions Menocal abandoned the presidency. One month later José Miguel Gómez died in New York.

During Menocal's eight years in office, for reasons more related to sugar than politics, Cuba had experienced profound transformations. In 1912 the price of sugar was 1.95 cents per pound, the lowest since the beginning of the century. The first world war and the almost total collapse of European sugar beet production changed the situation and opened a dazzling period of prosperity. After 1914 the price of sugar rose steadily, in 1920 reaching an astonishing 23 cents per pound. But then the price sank to 3.5 per pound. The 'dance of the millions' ended abruptly in bankruptcy and misery.

It is essential to note some of the consequences of this sugar boom. While in the thirteen years before the first world war only 15 sugar mills were constructed in Cuba, from 1914 to 1920 38 mills were built, most of them in the eastern region, converting Camagüey and Oriente into the island's most productive sugar zones. (Their percentage in Cuba's total production rose from 15 per cent in 1902 to 55 per cent in 1922.) As the cane production system used in Cuba was based on extensive planting instead of intensive cultivation, higher profits prompted sugar-mill owners to acquire as much land as possible, weakening *colonos* and transforming *latifundismo* into a formidable economic problem. Furthermore, to keep production costs low, hacendados fought every demand for better wages and resorted to the importation of cheap labour from Haiti and Jamaica, increasing social and racial tensions among peasants and workers. The sugar boom, and the absence of European competition, also intensified American penetration of the Cuban economy (US investments in Cuba rose from $205 million in 1911 to $1,200 million in

---

[21] Quoted in Louis A. Pérez, *Intervention, revolution, and politics in Cuba, 1913–1921* (Pittsburgh, 1978), 127.

1924), increased Cuba's dependence on the USA for its imports as well as sugar exports (51 per cent of Cuba's imports came from the USA in 1914, 83 per cent in 1915) and deepened the trend towards a single-crop economy.

All this explains why the collapse of 1920 had such devastating consequences. Almost all Cuban banks ran out of money, many Cuban-owned sugar mills had to be sold to foreigners, principally Americans, and every sector of the population felt the impact of the economic disaster. The *colono* system, which had been expanding since the end of the nineteenth century, creating what could be termed a rural middle class, suffered a terrible setback. It has been estimated that in the nine years following the crisis of 1921, out of a total of 50,000 *colonos* 18,000 lost their land. And the majority of the survivors became almost totally dependent on the will of the sugar mill owners.[22]

The crisis, however, had its positive results. Many Cubans became aware of their nation's vulnerability to external economic forces, and to the extent of American domination. By 1921, when Zayas assumed the presidency, the economic shock had revitalized Cuban nationalism and engendered a general demand for reforms. Public honesty, legislation to protect Cuban interests, diversification of agriculture, and a firm stand toward the United States became national issues. In 1922, Manuel Sanguily once more raised his voice to condemn the selling of Cuban lands to foreigners;[23] that same year a group of prominent Cubans proposed the creation of a National Bank, and in 1927 the most serious and influential criticism of *latifundismo* in Cuba was published, Ramiro Guerra y Sánchez's *Azúcar y población en las Antillas*. The emergence of a new generation of politicians added a radical, impatient accent to the protesting voices.

Alfredo Zayas, the new president 'elected' in 1921, in the middle of the crisis, was a cultivated, opportunistic lawyer almost totally free of moral scruples. At the moment when 'regeneration' was an increasingly fervent demand, he managed to downgrade Cuban politics to its lowest level. Initially, with the government tottering towards bankruptcy, Zayas had no alternative but to yield to Crowder's pressure for reforms. In June 1922 a new Cabinet, nicknamed the 'honest Cabinet', was formed under Crowder's watchful eye. Reduction of the national budget from $130

[22] Alberto Arredondo, *Cuba: tierra indefensa* (Havana, 1945), 333.

[23] See his last speeches in *Defensa de Cuba* (Havana, 1948), 146–9. As early as 1909 Sanguily had proposed a law, never approved by Congress, forbidding the selling of Cuban lands to foreigners.

million to $55 million, honest administration of the lottery system, and a serious effort to control public corruption were some of the accomplishments of the cabinet. Crowder's actions, however, provoked strong opposition in Cuba. In June 1922, even the usually pliable Congress adopted a resolution condemning Crowder's interventions in Cuban internal affairs, and reminding him of Elihu Root's original interpretation of the Platt Amendment, which rejected such interference. In 1923 the Zayas government received a loan of $50 million from the House of Morgan and Zayas felt free to exert his authority. Conveniently bowing to the prevalent nationalistic mood, he defied Crowder and dismantled the 'honest Cabinet'. By the middle of the year the old system of graft was back in force. Fortunately for Zayas, Crowder could do nothing to oppose this development. After his promotion to the rank of ambassador he had to follow Washington's new and more cautious policy, based on avoiding direct intervention or even openly pressuring the Cuban government for reforms. As Dwight Morrow, businessman and diplomat, told Crowder, 'good government is no substitute for self-government'.[24] Thus, Crowder was forced to keep a diplomatic silence.

The prevailing mood in Cuba, however, was no longer passive. Since 1922, inflamed by the proclamations of Argentinian students at the University of Córdoba (1918), and influenced by the 'anti-Yankee' feeling of most Latin American intellectuals (for example, José Vasconcelos in Mexico and Manuel Ugarte in Argentina) and the revolutionary events in Mexico, students at Havana University began demanding the forging of a 'new Cuba', free from corruption and Yankee tutelage. Martí's unfulfilled dream of a Republic 'with all and for the benefit of all' became the avowed goal of their efforts. A new and ardent love for Cuba and anguish at her condition appeared in dramas, novels, poems and popular music. Simultaneously young professionals and the leaders of the better organized labour organizations joined in the clamour for reforms. Even *colonos* and hacendados expressed dissatisfaction with prevalent conditions. Significantly, in 1923 a loose alliance of many of these groups formed a 'Veterans and Patriots Association' which published a programme for 'national reconstruction' that included the abrogation of the Platt Amendment, women's suffrage and workers' participation in business enterprises. Almost simultaneously, a

---

[24] Robert F. Smith, *The United States and Cuba: business and diplomacy, 1917–1960* (New Haven, 1960), 100. The author asserts that 'the State Department actually did not make a policy change . . . American business interests were satisfied, so there was no occasion for further action', *ibid.*, 101.

group of young intellectuals published a resounding 'Protest of the
Thirteen', condemning not only the Zayas administration's corruption,
but the entire Cuban political system. The support they received
surprised even the impassive Zayas. 'Times have changed', he confided
to senator Wifredo Fernández. But the president did not change.

In 1925, the Cuban Communist party was founded by old Labour
organizers like Carlos Baliño, student leaders like Julio Antonio Mella,
and several disenchanted ex-anarchists. Its direct influence was minimal,
but very soon Marxist concepts, probably not fully studied, appeared in
the writings of the new generation. As Joaquín Martínez Sáenz, a lawyer
and future revolutionary (he was the main organizer of ABC, an anti-
Machado secret organization), expressed it later: 'We were dazzled by the
apparent simplicity and clarity of Marxist theories . . . all Cuban
problems could be explained through class struggle and yankee
imperialism.'[25]

The new political atmosphere gave a special importance to the
forthcoming presidential elections. A revitalized Liberal party, with
General Gerardo Machado as its candidate, opposed ex-president
Menocal, once again the candidate of the Conservatives. The Liberal
campaign for 'regeneration' and Machado's 'honesty, roads and schools'
generated national enthusiasm. Probably bribed by Machado, Zayas
remained neutral, even though his party sided with the Liberals, assuring
honest elections. Machado won five of the six provinces. On 20 May
1925 he was sworn in as Cuba's fifth president.

A veteran of the War of Independence with a long but not very
distinguished political career, Machado was frank, energetic, and tough.
He firmly believed that only a strong hand could save Cuba from corrupt
politicians and never hesitated to use harsh methods whenever opposition stood in his way. The first two years of his term fulfilled many Cuban
hopes. The government was honest; legislation to protect Cuban
products, diversify agriculture and regulate the sugar industry was
promulgated, while a vast programme of public works and road
construction, including a central highway from Havana to Santiago de
Cuba, gave jobs to thousands of Cubans. Lining up behind the president,
the traditional political parties followed a policy of *cooperativismo* and
thereby transformed Congress into a docile institution. Without real
political opposition and amidst collective praise, Machado ruled as no

[25] Letter to the author, dated 18 January 1968. Typically, by 1934, Martínez Sáenz and most of his
generation had rejected Marxist ideas and clashed with the Communist party.

other Cuban president had before. Only small groups of students and some labour leaders criticized the government for increasing the public debt through new loans and applying brutal methods when dealing with strikers. The Nationalist Union formed by Colonel Carlos Mendieta and, to a certain extent, the recently founded Communist party (1925) were causes for government concern, but neither of these groups carried very much weight in 1927. The Nationalist Union was only a variation of Cuba's old traditional parties, and the Communists, guided by intellectuals and poets like Rubén Martínez Villena, had little influence among workers.

Propelled by his own political machinery and personal ambition, Machado took a clear step toward dictatorship in 1927. On the pretext of abolishing the right of presidential re-election, a pro-Machado, elected Constitutional Assembly extended presidential terms to six years and invited Machado to accept a new term in power. Then in 1928 Congress passed an Emergency Law prohibiting presidential nominations by any other than the Liberal, Conservative and Popular parties, which had all nominated Machado. After visiting the United States to obtain Washington's approval and playing host to the Sixth International Conference of American States held in Havana, on 1 November 1928 Machado was duly re-elected, unopposed, for a new six-year term.

The glaring unconstitutionality of the whole process and Machado's dictatorial methods aroused the opposition. Menocal came out of retirement to join Mendieta in condemning Machado's actions. Several distinguished political and intellectual figures such as Enrique José Varona strongly protested, and university students, mobilized by a newly formed Student Directory, appealed to the people to fight against a 'fascist' dictatorship. Undaunted, Machado answered with censorship and occasional brutality. In the summer of 1929 he boasted about his popular support and derided the opposition: it consisted of 'a group of corrupt politicians and a bunch of misguided kids'.

The Wall Street crash in October 1929 drastically altered the balance of forces in Cuba. In 1920–1 the slump in sugar prices had created a deep economic crisis in Cuba, but American loans and investments had helped to alleviate the situation. This time it was the American market which collapsed, dragging Cuba into an even worse economic crisis. Sugar production and sugar exports declined sharply. From 1928 to 1932 the price of sugar dropped from 2.18 cents per pound to an all-time low of 0.57 cents per pound. In 1929 tobacco exports amounted to $43,067,000;

in 1933 they only reached $13,861,000. Salaries and wages fell,
unemployment soared. And this time there were no palliatives.

The economic crisis eroded Machado's popularity and encouraged the
opposition openly to defy the regime. In 1930, after a political meeting in
Artemisa had ended in bloodshed, violence increased. By November
students had a martyr in Rafael Trejo who was killed in a confrontation
with the police, and an admiring national audience. Praise for the gallant
youths fighting against tyranny came from all sectors. In the meantime,
the traditional politicians who combined forces with Mendieta and
Menocal to fight Machado provoked the anger of the younger
generation by keeping close contacts with the American Embassy and
trying to obtain its open support. They were puzzled by Washington's
new policy of caution. The era of direct intervention, the landing of the
marines and blunt 'notes' from the State Department was coming to an
end. Washington now preferred to veil its intentions behind a cloud of
enigmatic words. When in October 1930, Secretary of State Henry L.
Stimson was asked if the American government would land forces in
Cuba, he summarized a vague answer with this cryptic phrase: 'every case
in the future will be judged on its merits and a situation might exist which
would distinguish it from the preceding ones'.[26]

Meanwhile, a different kind of political struggle agitated Cuba. In the
past, violence had been limited to sporadic clashes among political
groups, but now whole sectors of Cuban society, from workers to
lawyers, entered the struggle, and the most radical elements of the
opposition began to utilise a terrible new weapon: urban terrorism.
Terrorism, repression; more terrorism, more repression; the well-
known cycles of dictatorship followed their course in Cuba. In August
1931, adopting traditional tactics, Mendieta and Menocal attempted an
uprising in the interior of the island, supposedly co-ordinated with some
segments of Machado's army. Everything went wrong and the two
leaders were easily captured in Río Verde, a zone in Pinar del Río, which
gave its name to the episode.

Machado's relief was short lived. The failure of the old leaders allowed
the younger generation to move to the forefront and radicalized the
struggle. The ABC, a new secret revolutionary organization initially
formed by middle-class professionals, published a deep and serious
analysis of the causes of the Cuban crisis,[27] and spread fear in government

26 *Foreign relations of the United States, 1930* (Washington, DC), 11, 663–5.
27 The ABC programmes and manifestos can be consulted in *Doctrina del ABC* (Havana, 1942).
    Some of the most prominent young intellectuals of the period, like Jorge Mañach and Emeterio
    Santovenia, contributed to the formulation of the programme.

circles with bombs and terrorist attacks. In the background, the continuous decline of Cuban exports increased unemployment and misery. Barely able to pay the army, challenged by an increasing number of enemies, the situation of the government was extremely difficult. Yet Machado was far from defeated. At the beginning of 1933 the political situation in Cuba could be described as one of deadlock: official brutality had not been able to crush the opposition; the opposition had no realistic hope of toppling Machado. Consequently, the election of Franklin D. Roosevelt and his announcement of a 'good neighbour' policy towards Latin America filled Cuba with anxious expectations. Once again Washington's action were to become decisive.

Committed to a policy of non-intervention in Latin American affairs, President Roosevelt decided to send a special envoy to solve the Cuban crisis. In May 1933, Benjamin Sumner Welles, who had previous diplomatic experiences in the Dominican Republic, arrived in Havana as Ambassador Extraordinary. The essence of his mission was to seek a legal solution and avoid a revolution in Cuba which could jeopardize Roosevelt's new policy. Soon after his arrival, Welles offered his mediation to both government and opposition. With the exception of the Student Directory, which branded Sumner Welles as 'another pro-consul of Yankee imperialism', and the Communists (who naturally were not invited), all opposition groups, including ABC, accepted Welles's mediation. Increasingly convinced that Machado had to be removed, Welles began to favour the opposition by insisting on demands which could only weaken the president's power and convince the Cubans that Machado had lost US support.

On 27 July, finally aware of Welles's manoeuvres but still convinced that the ambassador was overstepping his instructions, Machado assured Congress that he would defend Cuba's sovereignty and asked for support against 'foreign intervention'. While the mediation evolved into a frontal confrontation between Welles and Machado, an unexpected event drastically altered the situation. On 4 August a minor strike of bus drivers developed into a general strike which paralysed Havana. Machado reached a compromise with Communist leaders to help him break the strike, but before any action could be taken, the announcement of his resignation by a clandestine radio station sent jubilant crowds to the streets. The inevitable bloody confrontation with the police doomed the government. The following day almost all activities ceased through-out the whole island. On 12 August, after some officers of the army rebelled, Machado bowed to the inevitable, resigned and abandoned the island. Immediately, Carlos M. Céspedes (son of the hero of the Ten Years' War) was sworn in as provisional president of the Republic.

In spite of Welles's support and the participation of ABC, Céspedes's government appeared too hesitant and restrained in a situation of economic crisis and revolutionary tension. On 4 September, taking advantage of the demoralization of the officer corps, the army sergeants rebelled, demanding better living conditions. Immediately the leaders of the Student Directory, who had denounced Céspedes's government as a tool of the Yankee ambassador, joined the rebellion and convinced the sergeants, by now commanded by Fulgencio Batista, to march on the presidential palace and depose Céspedes. As one of the actors wrote, they transformed 'a military uprising into an authentic revolution'.[28]

After an attempt to establish a ruling pentarchy, the students proclaimed Ramón Grau San Martín, a university professor, as president of the Republic. Though lasting only four months, this revolutionary government became the expression of most of the tensions and aspirations which had been growing in Cuba since the 1920s. With young Antonio Guiteras as its most dynamic leader, the government abrogated the Platt Amendment, proclaimed an agrarian reform, encouraged labour unions, gave the vote to women, curbed the power of American companies, and made it obligatory that 50 per cent of workers in all industries were Cubans. But it lacked a political party which could organize mass support, and had to face too many enemies. While the Communists, following the tactics of the Third International, attacked it as 'a lackey of Yankee imperialism', Sumner Welles used all his influence in Washington to convince President Roosevelt not to recognize the revolutionary government because it was too leftist and could not guarantee public order.

The revolutionary government could crush a futile attempt by ex-officers of the army to regain power, and a rebellion of ABC, but it could not restore order or calm the fear of many Cuban sectors (business and labour) about impending economic disaster if the US refused to buy the *zafra*. As the government's radicalism increased, the ranks of its followers dwindled. Internally divided, the Student Directory disbanded, and the sergeants, now colonels, became increasingly alarmed. By December, Batista, who had been in close contact with Sumner Welles,

---

[28] Enrique Fernández, *La razón del 4 de Septiembre* (Havana, 1950), 40. Six years later, the principal participants in this episode organized the Authentic party, which was to rule Cuba from 1944 to 1952.

was openly conspiring against the government. On 15 January 1934, in spite of Guiteras's desperate efforts to organize para-military units, Batista had mustered enough political backing to demand Grau's resignation. On 17 January, while Grau, Guiteras and many student leaders went into exile, Carlos Mendieta, an honest but very naive politician, was proclaimed president. Five days later, Ambassador Jefferson Caffery, who had substituted Sumner Welles in December, extended to the new government the official diplomatic recognition of the United States. That very year, a treaty between Cuba and the United States abrogated the Platt Amendment.

The turmoil of 1930–4, however, proved to be much more than another episode of political violence in Cuba. The nationalistic, social and political forces unleashed transformed the island and opened a new era. The leaders, parties and ideas which emerged in 1933 dominated and controlled the destinies of Cuba for the next 25 years. The Cuban society which Fidel Castro confronted in 1959, and even Castro's rise to power, cannot be understood without taking into account the profound impact that the frustrated revolution of 1933 had on the history of Cuba.

3

CUBA, *c.* 1930–1959

No part of Cuba escaped the ravages of the war with Spain that ended in 1898. From the eastern mountains across the central plains to the western valleys, the scene of desolation and devastation was the same. It was a brutal conflict in which the opposing armies seemed determined more to punish the land than prosecute the war, practising pillage of every kind for almost four years. More than 100,000 small farms, 3,000 livestock ranches and 700 coffee *fincas* were destroyed. Of the estimated 1,100 sugar mills registered in 1894, only 207 survived. Property-owners, urban and rural, were in debt and lacked either access to capital or sources of credit.

This devastation was neither unforeseen nor unplanned. In fact, it was the principal purpose for which Cubans, who understood well the political economy of colonialism, had taken up arms. It was indeed a war against property, and by 1898 separatist tactics had vindicated the goal of separatist strategy: Spain was on the brink of collapse. But the success of the Cuban military campaign did not produce the desired political results. Rather, it precipitated United States intervention, and at this point all the Cubans' plans went awry. They had thrown everything into the campaign against Spain. Victory over Spain left them exhausted, weak and vulnerable.

Armed intervention led to military occupation, at the end of which, in May 1902, the United States had effectively reduced Cuban independence to a mere formality. The Platt Amendment denied the new republic treaty-making authority, established limits on the national debt and sanctioned North American intervention for 'the maintenance of a government adequate for the protection of life, property and individual liberty'. The reciprocity treaty not only bound Cuba's principal export commodity, sugar, to a single market, the United States, but also opened key sectors of the Cuban economy – agriculture (especially sugar and tobacco), cattle-ranching, mining (especially iron), transportation (especially railways), utilities (gas, electricity, water, telephones) and banking – to foreign, mainly U.S., control.

By the beginning of the second decade of the twentieth century, whereas total British investments stood at $60 million, largely in telephones, railways, port works and sugar; French investments at $12 million, principally in railroads, banks and sugar; and German investments at $4.5 million, divided between factories and utilities; United States capital invested in Cuba exceeded $200 million. Under the reciprocity treaty preferential access to U.S. markets for Cuban agricultural products served to encourage Cuban dependency on sugar and, to a lesser extent, tobacco, and to increase foreign control over vital sectors of the economy. Reciprocity also discouraged economic diversification by promoting the consolidation of land from small units into the latifundia and concentration of ownership from local family to foreign corporation. And the effects of reciprocity were not confined to agriculture. The reduction of Cuban duties, in some instances as high as 40 per cent, opened the island to North American imports on highly favourable terms. The privileged access granted the U.S. manufacturers created a wholly inauspicious investment climate for Cuban capital. Even before 1903 the dearth of local capital and depressed economic conditions had combined to prevent development of national industry; after the reciprocity treaty prospects for local enterprise diminished further. North American manufactured goods saturated the Cuban market and hindered the development of local competition. Many firms could not compete with United States manufactures, and business failures increased.

Within a decade of the War of Independence the United States had become a pervasive presence in Cuba, totally dominating the economy, thoroughly penetrating the social fabric and fully controlling the political process. The ubiquity of this presence served to shape the essential character of the early republic.

Cuban politics acquired a distinctively distributive quality soon after independence. Because much of the national wealth rapidly passed into the hands of foreigners, political office guaranteed successful office-seekers and the retinue of their supporters access to the levers of resource and benefit allocation in the only enterprise wholly Cuban – government. Re-election violated the intra-elite protocol implicit in the electoral method of circulating public office. Monopolization of public office by one party, or one faction of a party, threatened to block access of others to the sinecures of state. Insofar as public administration under the republic served as a principal source of livelihood for the elites, elections institutionalized a process among power contenders by which participants shared, more or less equally, a guaranteed cyclical access to government. Indeed, so vital was the preservation of this system that the presidential succession precipitated armed protest in 1906, after the re-election of Tomás Estrada Palma, and again in 1917 against Mario G. Menocal.

Resistance to the re-election of President Gerardo Machado for a second term in 1928 came from the traditional Conservative and Popular parties, but also from within his own Liberal Party. In 1927, Carlos Mendieta broke with the party and established the Unión Nacionalista, openly opposed to presidential re-election. Other well-known party leaders, such as the disaffected Liberals Federico Laredo Bru and Roberto Méndez Peñate and the former Conservative president Mario G. Menocal, protested against re-electionism and fled into exile to organize opposition to Machado.

However, the challenge to the *machadato* did not originate principally from the established parties. New forces were stirring in Cuban society. By the 1920s the first republican-born generation of Cubans had reached political maturity and found the republic wanting. National disillusionment found expression first in the marketplace of ideas, in university reform, new literary and artistic currents, and fresh perspectives on history. Disillusionment gave way to disaffection as hopes for cultural regeneration fused with visions of political redemption. The political agenda expanded to include anti-imperialism, nationalism and social justice, but it was primarily against banality of national politics and the improbity of public officials that this generation directed its ire. In March 1923 radical intellectuals published a manifesto denouncing corruption in government. A month later the Junta de Renovación Nacional Cívica published a lengthy denunciation of graft, corruption and fraud. In August the veterans organization joined former officers of the old Liberation Army with dissident intellectuals to demand political and administrative reforms. Discontent spread to other sectors of society. In 1923, university students organized into the Federación Estudiantil Universitaria (FEU). Labour militancy increased as trade unions expanded at both provincial and national levels. In 1925, workers organized the Confederación Nacional Obrera de Cuba (CNOC), the first national labour organization. In that same year, the Cuban Communist Party (PCC) was founded.

Intellectuals, students and labour had pushed dissent beyond the limits of traditional partisan politics and into the realm of reform and revolution.

The very content of the national debate had changed. The republican generation was possessed of a peculiar redemptive mission, one that had as its goal the total regeneration of the republic – one, too, that challenged as much the assumptions upon which Machado governed as it did Machado's government.

Nevertheless, in 1927, through a combination of intimidation, coercion and bribery, Machado eventually secured the joint nomination of the traditional parties for a second term. *Cooperativismo,* as the arrangement became known, joined the Liberal, Conservative and Popular parties behind Machado's candidacy for re-election. More important, it ended all semblance of party independence and political competition, the traditional sources of anti-reelectionist violence. Later in 1927 Machado also secured congressional passage of a resolution amending the Constitution to extend the presidential term of office by two years. And in November 1928, unopposed as the *candidato único,* Machado won re-election to a new six-year term.

In many ways the re-election of Machado represented a collective response by the traditional political elites to the profound changes overtaking Cuban society. *Cooperativismo* was itself a necessary coalition among the embattled traditional parties designed to overcome the mounting challenge to the old order. For thirty years, the veterans of the nineteenth-century wars for independence had dominated the island's politics, bargaining among themselves political accommodations to ensure their continued pre-eminence. In 1928 this political community of interests found its logical conclusion in the *cooperativista* consensus. Indeed, *cooperativismo* promised to stabilize intra-elite politics at a time when the politicos were themselves under siege and facing the most serious challenge to their thirty-year rule of the republic.

The re-election of Machado in 1928 certainly served both to deepen opposition and give focus to dissent. But it was the world depression that accelerated political confrontation and intensified social conflict. Sugar production, the fulcrum upon which the entire Cuban economy balanced, dropped 60 per cent. In mid-1930 economic conditions deteriorated further when the United States enacted the Hawley–Smoot Tariff Act, a protectionist measure that increased duties on Cuban sugar. (The Cuban share of the U.S. market shrank from 49.4 per cent in 1930 to 25.3 per cent in 1933.) Sugar producers struggled to remain solvent by lowering wages and cutting production through labour lay-offs. The *zafra* was reduced to a sixty-two-day harvest, only two months' work for tens of thousands of sugar-workers. Some 250,000 heads of families, representing approximately 1 million people out of a total population of 3.9 million, found themselves totally unemployed. Those fortunate enough to escape total unemployment found temporary work difficult to come by and wages depressed. Pay for agricultural workers declined by 75 per cent, wages in the sugar zones falling as low as twenty cents a day. In some districts labourers received only food and lodging for their work. Wages for the urban proletariat decreased by 50 per cent as commercial, banking and manufacturing failures reached record proportions. In 1930 the government announced drastic salary cuts for all public employees except the armed forces, and the first of a series of redundancies in the state sector was imposed the following year. Members of the well-established middle class, particularly those professional groups that had traditionally found security and solvency in the civil service and public administration, were among the newest arrivals to augment the swelling ranks of the unemployed.

By 1930, as the full effects of the economic crisis reverberated across the island, virtually all sectors of Cuban society were at odds with the Machado government. In March 1930 a general strike organized by the outlawed CNOC and supported by 200,000 workers paralysed the island; in September a student anti-government protest resulted in violence and the closing of the university. As mass demonstrations spread, union membership expanded strikes halting production in key sectors of the economy including cigar-manufacturing, metallurgy, construction and textiles, in 1929 and 1930. The 1930 general strike ended only after fierce repression, arrests, torture and assassinations becoming commonplace. Increased repression did not, however, reduce resistance. On the contrary, opposition to Machado increased. A desultory warfare broke out in the countryside, the torching of canefields destroying millions of *arrobas* of cane. Armed bands operated throughout the interior, ambushing trains, cutting telephone and telegraph wires and attacking isolated Rural Guard posts. In November 1930, the government proclaimed a state of siege throughout the island. Army units in full combat dress assumed police functions in provincial cities and towns. Military supervisors displaced civilian governors in Pinar del Río, Matanzas, Las Villas, Camagüey and Oriente, and army tribunals superseded civilian courts. Constitutional guarantees were restored on 1 December but suspended again ten days later. Repression depended upon an extensive police apparatus: a secret police was organized – the Sección de Expertos, specialists in the method of torture – while the Partida de la

Porra served as a government death squad. Cuba assumed the appearance of an armed camp under a regime for which neutrality was suspect and the slightest criticism was subversive.

The organized opposition responded in kind, several groups taking up arms to challenge Machado. The ABC consisted of intellectuals, professionals and students, organized in clandestine cells and committed to creating conditions of revolution through systematic use of violence against the government. The Organización Celular Radical Revolucionaria (OCRR) also adopted a cellular structure and adopted armed struggle and sabotage as the means to overthrow Machado. In 1931 an ideological dispute within the Directorio Estudiantil Universitario (DEU) resulted in the formation of the Ala Izquierda Estudiantil (AIE) which, dedicated to the radical transformation of Cuban society, formed 'action squads' of urban guerrillas and carried the struggle into the streets. The PCC expanded its revolutionary activities as well as asserting leadership over key trade unions, most notably CNOC. In 1932, sugar-workers established the first national union, the Sindicato Nacional Obrero de la Industria Azucarera (SNOIA) while women's resistance groups, university professors, and normal-school teachers and students joined an underground network dedicated to armed struggle against Machado. By the early 1930s, the crisis was moving beyond a political settlement. As economic conditions deteriorated and social unrest spread, the struggle against Machado was changing daily into a movement seeking more to overturn a system rather than overthrow a president.

In 1933 Cuba quivered at the brink of revolution. Sixty per cent of the population lived at submarginal levels of under $300 in annual real income; another 30 per cent earned marginal wages between $300 and $600. Early in the year exiled opposition leaders organized into a revolutionary junta in New York and called for a national revolution to remove Machado. The Cuban ambassador to Washington acknowledged privately to the State Department that the beleaguered Machado government faced serious political trouble and appealed to the new Democratic administration for immediate U.S. support. Otherwise, he predicted somberly, 'chaos would result, the sort of chaos that might easily require the United States to intervene in a military way'.[1] However, Washington

---

[1] William Phillips, 'Memorandum of Conversation with Cuban Ambassador', 5 May 1933, File 550 S.S. Washington/415, General Records of the Department of State, Record Group 59, National Archives, Washington, D.C. (hereinafter cited as RG 59).

was unwilling to entertain the idea of armed intervention in 1933. Having committed his administration to a Latin American policy based on the notion of a 'good neighbour', Franklin Roosevelt was unwilling to inaugurate a new phase in hemispheric relations by sending troops to Cuba. Washington favoured instead a negotiated political settlement in which Machado would resign before the expiration of his term in 1935, thereby permitting a coalition of moderate political groups to form a provisional government.

Developments in Cuba concerned the United States in another way. The U.S. was also concerned by the fact that its grip over the Cuban economy was slipping. In the three decades since the signing of the reciprocity treaty, a series of developments had altered U.S.–Cuban trade patterns. The tariff law of 1927 launched Cuba on an import substitution program, increasing self-sufficiency in a variety of products formerly imported, including eggs, butter, lard, shoes, furniture and hosiery. U.S. exports to Cuba also suffered from increased foreign competition as the depression and the drop of Cuba's purchasing power combined to make the island a price market and opened the door to the importation of cheap commodities from Europe and Japan previously supplied by the United States on a quality basis.

The effects were substantial. Between 1923 and 1933, Cuban imports from the United States declined from $191 million to $22 million while Cuban exports to the United States decreased from $362 million to $57 million. The U.S. share in Cuban imports diminished from 74.3 per cent during the First World War to 66.7 per cent in 1922 and 61.8 per cent in 1927. By 1933 it had decreased to 53.5 per cent, and Cuba had dropped from sixth to sixteenth place as a customer for U.S. exports. The U.S. Department of Agriculture estimated that the loss of Cuban markets for foodstuffs alone meant the withdrawal of 817,267 acres from agricultural production in the United States. Exports to Cuba of raw materials and manufactured products other than foodstuffs dropped from $133 million in 1924 to $18 million in 1933.

The purpose of U.S. policy in Cuba, thus, was twofold: first, to end conditions of political instability and, second, to recover control over Cuban markets. To these ends the State Department appointed Sumner Welles as ambassador to Cuba. Welles' instructions directed him to offer the 'friendly mediations' of the United States for the purpose of securing a 'definite, detailed, and binding understanding' between the government and the opposition.[2] And early in June, Welles secured the agreement of the government parties and moderate opposition, including the ABC, OCRR and the Unión Nacionalista, to participate in discussion.

Through the early summer the actual purpose of Welles' mission to Havana remained unknown and undisclosed. Methodically and patiently, Welles maneouvred the mediations towards the twin objectives of persuading Machado to resign and thus bring the Cuban political crisis to a peaceful conclusion. Yet these were only the means. The objective was to end the revolutionary threat to the institutional structures upon which Cuban elites ruled, and upon which U.S. hegemony rested, and to establish a government in Cuba that would renegotiate a new reciprocity treaty, thereby restoring North American primacy in Cuban's foreign commerce. 'The negotiation at this time of a reciprocal trade agreement with Cuba . . .', Wells wrote from Havana, 'will not only revivify Cuba but will give us practical control of a market we have been steadily losing for the past ten years not only for our manufactured products but for our agricultural exports'.[3]

Machado had outlived his usefulness. The order and stability which he had provided during his first term, and which had won Washington's support for his re-election, had collapsed. The anti-Machado struggle had stepped beyond the bounds of conventional political competition and generalized into a revolutionary situation. After nearly five years of sustained civil strife it had become apparent that Machado could not restore order. His continued presence was now the greatest single obstacle to the restoration of order and stability. In late July, Welles informed the unsuspecting President that a satisfactory solution to the crisis required him to shorten his term by one year. Machado responded first with incredulity and then with rage. He convened a special session of Congress to repudiate the proposed settlement, vowing to remain in power through his full term of office.

In the days that followed, Welles worked to undermine Machado's domestic support as a means of forcing him into early retirement. If Machado fell solely through North American pressure, the traditional political parties, discredited by their collaboration with Machado, faced the prospect of drastic reorganization, at best, or complete suppression – as many opposition factions demanded. The success of an internal revolt

---

[2] Cordell Hull to Sumner Welles, 1 May 1933, U.S. Department of State, *Foreign Relations of the United States, 1933*, 5 vols. (Washington, D.C. 1941), 5:285.
[3] Sumner Welles to Cordell Hull, 13 May, 1933, 833.00/3512, DS/RG 59.

against the government similarly threatened the old party structure with extinction by subjecting Machado supporters to political reprisals from the regime's opponents. Support for the ambassador's recommendations, however, carried some assurances that the parties would survive the *machadato*. In early August, therefore, the leaders of the Liberal, Conservative and Popular parties endorsed the mediator's proposals and introduced in Congress legislation designed to expedite Machado's departure.

Welles moved next against the diplomatic underpinnings of the Cuban government and threatened Machado with the withdrawal of North American support. He insisted that under the terms of the Platt Amendment, Machado had simply failed to maintain a government adequate for the protection of life, property and individual liberty. The continuation of these conditions, Welles warned Machado, would require U.S. intervention. To Washington, Welles recommended the withdrawal of diplomatic recognition if, at the end of a reasonable period, Machado continued to resist early retirement. He assured the State Department that this would obviate the necessity of an armed intervention by making it impossible for Machado to survive in power much longer.

In mid-summer the struggle between the U.S. ambassador and the Cuban President assumed a new urgency. On 25 July bus drivers in Havana organized a strike in protest against a new government tax. Within a week a clash between the protesting drivers and the police resulted in sympathy strikes among taxi drivers, streetcar operators and truck drivers. The transportation strike in the capital spread to other sectors and within days all movement of people and goods came to a halt. By the end of the first week of August, the general strike had acquired the full proportions of a revolutionary offensive and Welles and Machado had acquired a much more formidable adversary that threatened to sweep aside both the regime of Machado and U.S. hegemony.

Machado and Welles recognized the gravity of the strike and turned immediately to defuse the deepening revolutionary situation. Each took extraordinary steps to end the strike. Machado conferred with the leadership of the PCC and CNOC, offering the party legality and the CNOC recognition in exchange for their support in ending the strike. It was an opportunity seized by the Communist Party. Under the terms of the agreement, the government released labour leaders and Communists from prison and proclaimed the legality of the PCC upon the end of the strike. The party leadership, in return, issued return-to-work orders. In fact, however, both Machado and the PCC misjudged conditions. The govern-

ment believed the party controlled the strike; the PCC believed the government to be stronger than it was. But the strike had evolved beyond the
Communist control and the government was beyond salvation.

For Welles, Machado's departure could no longer wait until May 1934,
the date set for the President's early retirement. His resignation was
required immediately. The ambassador would later recall that the 'omi-
nous signs provided by a paralyzing strike' necessitated a 'radical solution'
to the Cuban problem to 'forestall the cataclysm which otherwise was
inevitable'.[4] On 11 August, Welles reported a confidential talk with
Secretary of War and former army chief General Alberto Herrera in which
he offered Herrera the presidency in exchange for his support in a quick
resolution of the crisis. This arrangement was a direct invitation to the
armed forces to impose a political settlement.

The army was already predisposed to act. Indeed, the armed forces had a
considerable stake in the outcome of the political conflict. The mediations
had not inspired confidence within the high command while rising anti-
militarism among the opposition had contributed to a general restlessness
among the officer corps. Opposition groups used the negotiations as a
forum to denounce the military, the ABC advocating a reduction in the
size of the military establishment and restrictions on army authority. One
report circulating throughout Havana suggested that the opposition
planned to reduce the army from 12,000 to 3,000 officers and men.
Business and professional groups, troubled by the excessive taxation required to support the military, similarly advocated reductions in the army.
As a result, army intervention in August 1933 was not unconditional. The
armed forces acted only after having secured in advance assurances from
opposition leaders, to which Welles subscribed, that the subsequent government would respect the integrity of the military. A 'strictly confidential' memorandum pledged that the armed forces would be maintained
without any alteration until 20 May 1935, the scheduled expiration of
Machado's second term. The proviso further stipulated that 'members of
the said armed forces . . . cannot be removed from their positions nor
punished' in any way inconsistent with the existing laws.[5]

On 12 August, the army demanded and secured Machado's resignation.

[4] Sumner Welles, *Two Years of the 'Good Neighbor' Policy.* Department of State, Latin American Series No. 11 (Washington, D.C., 1935), pp. 8–9.
[5] 'Memorandum', 11 August 1933, enclosure in Orestes Ferrara to Sumner Welles, 12 August 1933, File (1933) 800, U.S. Embassy, Cuba, Correspondence, Record Group 84, Records of the Foreign Service Posts of the United States, U.S. National Archives, Washington, D.C.

Herrera's succession was, however, resisted on grounds that the Secretary of War was too closely identified with the fallen president. Undeterred, Welles continued to pursue an orderly and constitutional resolution of the crisis. All *machadista* cabinet members except Herrera resigned. Herrera then served as provisional president only long enough to appoint as Secretary of State Carlos Manuel de Céspedes, who was something of a political non-entity – or 'statesman', as he loftily described himself – an inoffensive compromise candidate who lacked affiliation with any political party or political tendency. Herrera then resigned to permit Céspedes to succeed as president.

The Céspedes government set in sharp relief the contradictions generated during the *machadato*. The Welles mediations had served to legitimize the formerly outlawed anti-Machado groups and guarantee their inclusion in the new government. On the other hand, the timely desertion of the dictator by the former government parties guaranteed them a political role in post-Machado Cuba. The distribution of government portfolios to representatives of such diverse factors as the ABC, the Liberal Party, the Unión Nacionalista, the Conservative Party, the OCRR and the Partido Popular, previously implacable adversaries, served to institutionalize the unresolved disputes of the *machadato*.

The difficulties confronting the new government were not, however, confined to internal contradictions. The departure of Machado had produced an immediate halt to government repression, and the change of governments clearly reduced national tensions and eased mounting revolutionary pressures. But Cuba remained in the throes of the depression, and the social and economic dislocations that had plunged the *machadato* into crisis continued unabated after 12 August. Strikes persisted as the new mood of labour militancy extended across the island. The organizations that had earlier boycotted the mediations – principally those sectors of the anti-Machado opposition that aspired to something more than simply a change of presidents – found the Céspedes solution wholly unsatisfactory. Many of these groups, including the two student organizations, the DEU and the AIE, and the Communist Party, had toiled too long in the pursuit of revolution to settle for a palace coup as the denouement of their political labour.

There were other problems for Céspedes. Public order had broken down. The rioting produced by Machado's flight continued intermittently through August, the mobs dispensing revolutionary justice to suspected *machadista* officials. Army and police authorities, formerly the object of popular enmity, now moved to control civilian excesses only tentatively, if at all. Many officers feared that strict enforcement of order under Céspedes would serve only to revive anti-army sentiment among those former opposition groups now in power. This military morale was in any case at a low level. Senior officers lived in fear of arrest and reprisals for their part in the *machadato* while junior officers eagerly awaited the promotions certain to follow the purge of *machadista* commanders. Non-commissioned officers and enlisted men grew increasingly restive as rumours foretold of impending pay cuts and troop reductions.

The end of the Céspedes government came from a most improbable and unexpected source. On the evening of 3 September sergeants, corporals and enlisted men of Camp Columbia in Havana met to discuss their grievances, the deliberations ending with the preparation of a list of demands to be submitted to the commanding officers. The officers on duty, however, declined to discuss the demands of the aroused soldiery and instead retired from the army post. Suddenly, and unexpectedly, the troops found themselves in control of Camp Columbia and in mutiny. The NCO protesters, under the leadership of Sergeant Fulgencio Batista, exhorted the troops to hold the post until the army command agreed to review their demands.

The soldiers' protest immediately received support from anti-government groups. In the early hours of 4 September, student leaders of the DEU arrived at Camp Columbia and persuaded the sergeants to expand the movement. Civilian intervention changed the nature of the NCO protest and transformed a mutiny into a putsch. The 'sergeants' revolt', as the mutiny later became known, was originally possessed of less ambitious objectives. The sergeants planned a demonstration only to protest against service conditions, specifically poor pay, inadequate housing facilities and rumoured cuts in the enlisted ranks – not the ouster of the officer corps or the overthrow of Céspedes. Having unexpectedly found themselves in a state of mutiny, and effectively in rebellion against the government, there was little enthusiasm to return to the barracks under the existing regime. The students offered an alternative. It was a coalition of convenience, not without flaw, but one that offered rebellious troops absolution and dissident civilians political power. Out of this tentative civil–military consensus emerged a revolutionary junta composed of Ramón Grau San Martín, Porfirio Franca, Guillermo Portela, José Irizarri and Sergio Carbó.

The transfer of the revolutionary junta from the Camp Columbia barracks to the presidential palace served to shift the locus of authority in Cuba. Power passed to those forces long situated at the fringes of the republican polity – radicals and nationalists – who saw themselves as the agents of a historical imperative as well as the instruments of a popular mandate. On the morning of 5 September, a political manifesto announced the establishment of a new Provisional Revolutionary Government and proclaimed the affirmation of national sovereignty, the establishment of a modern democracy and the 'march toward the creation of a new Cuba'.

The forces of old Cuba responded with more than indignation to the September usurpation. The established government parties that earlier had deserted Machado as a means to survive the discredited regime once again faced persecution and extinction. So too did the ousted *machadista* army officers who, for all their efforts to secure immunity from post-Machado reprisals, now found themselves vulnerable to prosecution and imprisonment. Representatives of business and commercial sectors recoiled in horror at the change of governments and openly predicted the collapse of the Cuban economy. Nor was it only old Cuba which opposed the revolutionary junta. New political groups, including the ABC and the OCRR, organizations that previously had paid dearly to attain political power in post-Machado Cuba, faced an abrupt and inglorious end to their debut in national politics. A government composed of radical students and created by mutinous soldiers had the immediate effect of uniting in opposition those political forces which had earlier been rivals in power.

The provisional government faced its most formidable adversary in the person of Sumner Welles, the U.S. ambassador. The coup had undermined constitutional legality and overthrown conservative authority, both of which had been arduously defended by Welles. The ambassador was neither slow to react nor unequivocal in his response. His immediate recourse was to recommend, unsuccessfully, U.S. military intervention in order to restore Céspedes to power. Welles deliberately characterized the new government in terms calculated to arouse suspicion and provoke opposition in Washington. The army had fallen under 'ultra-radical control', Welles cabled Washington, and the government was 'frankly communistic'. Irizarri was characterized as a 'radical of the extreme type' while Grau and Portela were described as 'extreme radicals'.[6]

---

[6] Sumner Welles to Secretary of State, 5 September 1933, 837.00/3757, RG 59, and 'Memorandum of Telephone Conversation Between Secretary of State Hull and Welles', 5 September 1933, 837.00/3800, RG 59.

Early opposition to the provisional government produced a number of immediate changes. In mid-September, the junta dissolved in favor of a more traditional executive form of government under Ramón Grau San Martín. Fear that the combination of political intrigue and disarray in the army command would result in the collapse of public order prompted the government to promote Fulgencio Batista to the rank of colonel and appoint him as army chief. He was instructed to commission new officers in sufficient numbers to maintain stability in the armed forces. In early October, the government proclaimed the former officers deserters and ordered their arrest, thereby paving the way for a total reorganization of the army under Batista. This certainly strengthened the position of the provisional government. But the purge of the old officer corps was also a political triumph for the army and a personal victory for Fulgencio Batista. And this deepened the contradictions within the provisional government. Students and soldiers remained inextricably bound together in the original transgression against constituted authority, and they shared mutual interests in the fortune of the provisional government, if only because they shared a common fate if it failed. Nevertheless, the gap between them widened after 4 September. The students carried Cuba into the realm of experimental government, not least because this was the first administration of the republic not formed with Washington's support. Reform proved to be intoxicating, and for one hundred days the students devoted themselves with exalted purposefulness to the task of transforming the country. Under the injunction of 'Cuba for Cubans', the new government proceeded to enact reforms laws at a dizzying pace, committing itself to economic reconstruction, social change and political reorganization. The new government abrogated the Platt Amendment and dissolved all the *machadista* parties. Utility rates were lowered by 40 per cent and interest rates reduced. Women received the vote and the university secured autonomy. In labour matters, government reforms included minimum wages for cane-cutters, compulsory labour arbitration, an eight-hour day, workers' compensation, the establishment of a Ministry of Labour, and a Nationalization of Labour decree requiring that 50 per cent of all employees in industry, commerce and agriculture be Cuban nationals. In agricultural affairs, the government sponsored the creation of *colono* associations, guaranteed peasants permanent right over land they occupied and inaugurated a program of agrarian reform.

As the students continued to advance on their 'march to create a new Cuba', the army became an increasingly reluctant escort. Military support of the provisional government was always more an expression of self-interest than a function of solidarity. This was the government that had sanctioned the sergeants' sedition and validated hundreds of new commissions, a government from which the new army command derived its legitimacy. But it was also true that the new leaders of the army were anxious for an immediate political settlement, if for no other reason than to institutionalize their recent gains. The army command saw little to be gained by social experimentation except a prolongation of uncertainty. Indeed, many *septembrista* commanders perceived the student projects as hazardous ventures, ill-conceived programs of a government upon whose solvency they depended to legitimize ill-gotten commissions.

These fears were skillfully exploited by Welles. By mid-autumn, he shifted his attention away from promoting unity among anti-government factions to encouraging division among its supporters. An astute observer of Cuban politics, Welles was well aware of the deepening contradictions within the provisional government. The sergeants' revolt, Welles reminded Washington, did 'not take place in order to place Grau San Martín in power'. He added that the 'divergence between the Army and civilian elements in the government is fast becoming daily more marked' and as Batista's influence grew 'the power of the students and Grau San Martín diminished'.[7] Another political coalition, Welles reasoned, one capable of constituting itself into legitimate government and willing to ratify the *septembrista* army command, could persuade Batista to abandon the government that had originally conferred military legitimacy on an army mutiny.

For the second time in as many months, Welles appealed directly to the army to overturn a government that had fallen into North American disfavour. On 4 October, days after the arrest of the former officers, the ambassador reported having had a 'protracted and very frank discussion' with Batista. Now characterizing Batista as the 'only individual in Cuba today who represented authority', Welles informed the army chief that he had earned the support of 'the very great majority of the commercial and financial interests in Cuba who are looking for protection and who could only find such protection in himself'. Political factions that only weeks earlier had openly opposed him, Welles explained, were now 'in accord that his control of the Army as chief of staff should be continued as the only possible solution and were willing to support him in that capacity'.

---

[7] Sumner Welles to Secretary of State, 5 October 1933, 837.00/4131, RG 59.

However, the only obstacle to an equitable arrangement, and presumably recognition and a return to normality, the ambassador suggested, 'was the unpatriotic and futile obstinacy of a small group of young men who should be studying in the university instead of playing politics and of a few individuals who had joined with them for selfish motives'. In a thinly veiled warning, Welles had reminded Batista of the tenuous position in which affiliation with the government placed him: 'should the present government go down in disaster, that disaster would necessarily inextricably involve not only himself but the safety of the Republic, which he had publicly pledged himself to maintain'.[8]

Welles' comments could not have been interpreted by Batista in any other fashion than an invitation to create a new government. There meetings served also to underscore the uncertainty of Batista's position. Non-recognition continued to encourage opposition and resistance. There remained a danger that a revolt would topple the provisional government and lead to the nullification of the *septembrista* army command and arrest of the former sergeants. Nor had prospects of a U.S. military intervention entirely passed, further raising the possibility that the United States would return Céspedes to power. Batista's authority within the armed forces was also threatened by his continued support of a government diplomatically opposed abroad and politically isolated at home. His command over the army rested on the sanction of a provisional government facing an uncertain future. Batista was simply one of four hundred recently promoted non-commissioned officers whose rank and appointment depended on a political settlement in Havana compatible with – or at least not hostile to – the new army hierarchy. As long as the *septembrista* officers remained identified with a government lacking legitimacy and deprived of the authority to underwrite permanently the promotions of 4 September, they risked sharing the ultimate fate of a regime opposed at home and abroad. Batista's own position within the army depended on his ability to legitimize the new commissions through a political settlement satisfactory to organized political and economic groups and Washington.

The end was not long in coming. In December, Welles reported with some satisfaction that Batista was actively seeking a change in government owing to his apprehension of a conspiracy within the army, the persistence of anti-government intrigue and fear of a North American intervention. In

[8] Ibid.

January 1934, Batista withdrew army support from Grau and backed the old disaffected Liberal politician, Carlos Mendieta. Within five days, the United States recognized Mendieta. Supported diplomatically abroad and with established political backing at home, the new government moved immediately to ratify the new army commissions. Decree Number 408 formally dissolved the old National Army and proclaimed in its place the newly organized Constitutional Army. The new army was to consist of all officers, non-commissioned officers and enlisted men on active duty at the time the decree was promulgated.

The forces of change released during the *machadato* did not abate with the passing of the Grau government. On the contrary, they found new forms of expression. The ancien regime had certainly found renewed life in new army chief Batista and old Liberal leader Mendieta, but not without renewed challenge. Most immediately, the reform program of the short-lived provisional government acquired institutional vitality with the organization in 1934 of the Partido Revolucionario Cubano (PRC/Auténtico) while, under the leadership of Antonio Guiteras, formerly Grau's minister of government, radicals formed a clandestine revolutionary organization, Joven Cuba. Eschewing electoral politics, Joven Cuba adopted armed struggle as the principal means to combat the Batista–Mendieta government. Assassination, bombings and sabotage again became the dominant mode of political opposition. Student opposition resumed with the reopening of the University of Havana in 1934. Anti-government demonstrations and labour protests once again became commonplace. Between 1934 and 1935 more than one hundred strikes flared up across the island.

In March 1935 momentum for revolutionary change assumed formidable proportions when an anti-government general strike plunged the island into crisis. Unlike August 1933, however, the government was neither willing to negotiate with labour nor reluctant to persecute participants. Proclamation of martial law announced a reign of terror that lasted through late spring. Strike leaders were arrested, many were tortured and assassinated, others fled into exile. Unions were outlawed and the university was occupied. In the weeks that followed military firing squads executed civilian dissidents. In May 1935 the army killed Antonio Guiteras.

The 1935 general strike was the last revolutionary surge of the republican generation. It collapsed after only a few days but its effects lasted through the decade. Most immediately, the severity of the military repression caused dissension in and then the dissolution of the ruling coalition. By the end of March, Mendieta found his support reduced to his own faction in the Unión Nacionalista and the military. Within months, he too, resigned. In a very real sense then, the strike achieved its desired effect but did not accomplish its principal objective. The Mendieta government did indeed collapse but in so doing created a political vacuum filled by Batista and the armed forces. Virtually every branch of government passed under army control. Military supervisors replaced provincial and municipal officials, the army command purging striking civil servants and establishing control over every division of public administration. The army emerged as the most important source of patronage and public employment. Batista was now the single most dominant political force on the island.

Batista's prestige increased throughout the 1930s as he restored order and stability. Washington found in the Pax Batistiana sufficient cause to continue diplomatic support for the dictator's puppet presidents and shadow governments: José A. Barnet (1935–6), Miguel Mariano Gómez (1936), and Federico Laredo Bru (1936–40). Nor did Batista's opponents of the 1930s recover. The tempest of the decade had blown itself out. Many of the most prominent opponents of the Batista–Mendieta regime had lost their lives in 1935. Others sought personal security in exile or departed Cuba to carry the banner of revolution to other lands, most notably Spain. Revolutionary groups had been shattered and crushed. When the university reopened in 1937 classes resumed uneventfully. The PRC/Auténtico turned to electoral politics and devoted itself to the arduous work of constructing a new party infrastructure and developing grassroots support. Moreover, by the end of the decade, the Communisty Party had made peace with Batista. After 1938, the party adopted a reformist and openly collaborationist posture, consolidating control over the trade unions and gaining legal status in exchange for political support of the Batista-backed government. Its newspaper was published and distributed publicly, and by the late 1930s the party appeared on the electoral rolls. Communist control over the trade-union movement expanded, culminating in 1939 with the establishment of the Confederación de Trabajadores Cubanos (CTC).

In some measure the restoration of social tranquillity was due to the programs pursued by the new army command. Certainly Batista transformed the Cuban army into an effective apparatus of repression. At the same time, however, the military leadership practised graft and corruption on a scale previously unknown in Cuba although Batista himself was interested in more than either political power or personal wealth. He committed the armed forces to a wide range of social programmes, starting in 1937 with the inauguration of the civic-military school system, under which sergeants served as schoolmasters throughout the countryside. These *misiones educativas*, designed to disseminate information concerning agriculture, hygiene and nutrition to rural communities, inaugurated a rudimentary education network in the interior. The army operated a thousand schools in which day sessions were devoted to the education of children and evenings to adults. By the late 1930s the army command had created an extensive military bureaucracy assigned exclusively to the administration of social programmes. A Three Year Plan was inaugurated to reform agriculture, education, public health and housing. One important effort of this was to provide the programmatic basis for Batista's direct entry into national politics at the end of the decade.

Economic conditions improved through the 1930s. Gradually Cuban sugar recovered a larger share of the U.S. market, although it would never again attain the prominence it enjoyed during the late 1910s and early 1920s. Under the terms of the Jones–Costigan Act of 1934 the United States lowered the protectionist tariffs on sugar imports, substituting quotas for tariff protection as the means to aid domestic sugar producers. The law empowered the U.S. Secretary of Agriculture to determine the annual sugar needs of the nation, whereupon all sugar-producing regions, domestic and foreign, would receive a quota of the total, which was based on the participation of sugar producers in the U.S. market for the years 1931–3. The selection of these years was unfortunate for Cuban producers, for it was precisely this period – the years of Hawley Smoot – in which the Cuban share of the U.S. market was the smallest. Nevertheless, the Cuban participation in the U.S. market increased slightly from 25.4 per cent in 1933 to 31.4 per cent in 1937. These were years, moreover, in which Cuban overall sugar production expanded, and the value of the expanded production increased. Between 1933 and 1938, Cuban sugar output increased from 1.9 million tons to 2.9 million tons, with the corresponding value increasing from 53.7 million pesos to 120.2 million pesos.

This slow economic revival, no less than the slight restoration of the Cuban share of the U.S. market, was not without a price. Under the terms of the new 1934 reciprocity treaty negotiated by the Mendieta govern-

ment, Cuba secured a guaranteed market for its agricultural exports in
return for tariff reductions to a large variety of commodity lines and the
reduction of internal taxes on U.S. products. Concessions granted by the
United States covered thirty-five articles; Cuban concessions affected four
hundred items. Tariff reductions granted to Cuban items ranged from 20
per cent to 50 per cent; tariff concessions to U.S. products ranged from 20
per cent to 60 per cent. The new agreement also specified that the enumer-
ated tariff schedule could not be altered as a result of changing money and
currency values.

The new treaty certainly contributed to Cuban revival since the country's principal export, sugar, was the item most favored by the 1934
agreement. The U.S. tariff on Cuban raw sugar was reduced from \$1.50 to
90 cents per pound. Reductions were also made on tobacco leaf as well as
cigars and cigarettes, honey, fish, products, citrus, pineapples and other
agricultural goods. At the same time, however, the 1934 treaty dealt a
severe blow to Cuban efforts at economic diversification. Scores of agricultural and manufacturing enterprises, many of which had arisen in the
aftermath of the 1927 customs-tariff law, were adversely affected. More
broadly, the new treaty allowed U.S. trade adjustment to changing market
conditions in Cuba, and ultimately re-established U.S. primacy in the
Cuban economy. Cuba was again linked closely to the United States,
thereby returning the island to the patterns of pre-depression dependency.
The total value of North American imports increased from \$22.6 million
in 1933 to \$81 million in 1940; the U.S. portion of Cuban imports for the
same period increased from 53.5 per cent to 76.6 per cent.

The renegotiation of the reciprocity treaty was accompanied by the
renegotiation of the Permanent Treaty, the legal form of the Platt Amendment. With the exception of provisions for United States use of the
Guantánamo naval station, the long-standing affrontery to Cuban national
sensibilities was removed. Henceforth, U.S.-Cuban relations would be
conducted formally between 'independent though friendly states'.

By the end of the decade, the passing of the economic crisis and the return
of political stability, particularly with acceptance of electoral politics by
the Auténticos and the Communist Party, created a climate auspicious for
constitutional reform. Batista's political position was firmly established
and could only be enhanced by his identifying himself with the demands
for reform. Indeed many of the measures enacted by the ill-starred Grau
government continued to enjoy considerable national popularity. Further-

more, the old Constitution of 1901 remained permanently stigmatized in Cuba since it contained as an organic part the odious Platt Amendment. Hence, a new constitution promised to make a break with the past and institutionalize the gains of post-Machado Cuba.

A constituent assembly representing the full spectrum of political affiliation, from old *machadistas* to the PRC and Communists, convened in 1939 to draft a new constitution. It provided the forum for renewed debate over virtually all the key issues of republican politics. Nor did political alignments determine the direction of the debates. The pro-government coalition included the discredited Liberals and moribund Unión Nacionalista as well as the Communist Party. The opposition was led by the Auténticos and included the ABC and supporters of former president Miguel Mariano Gómez. Thus, ideology tended to transcend partisan affiliation, left-liberal delegates frequently joining forces to form voting majorities against conservatives, without regard to affiliation with government or opposition blocs. The net result was the promulgation in 1940 of a remarkably progressive constitution which provided for the use of referendum, universal suffrage and free elections and which sanctioned a wide range of political and civil liberties. The charter's social provisions included maximum hours and minimum wages, pensions, workers' compensation, the right to strike and state guarantees against unemployment.

For all its enlightened clauses, the Constitution of 1940 remained substantially a statement of goals, an agenda for future achievement. The absence of provisions for enforcement meant that the new Constitution would remain largely unrealized. At the same time, it soon occupied a place of central importance in national politics since it served alternately as the banner through which to mobilize political support and the standard by which to measure political performance. Many of the objectives of the 1930s found vindication in the new Constitution, which also provided the foundations for legitimacy and consensus politics for the next twelve years. Cuban politics would henceforth turn on partisan promises to interpret most faithfully and implement most vigorously the principal clauses of the Constitution.

The promulgation of the new constitution also set the stage for the celebration of presidential elections in 1940. Batista stepped out of uniform and Grau San Martín returned from exile to challenge his old rival. The campaign was vigorously waged, and the election was certainly among the most honest in the nearly four decades at the republic's history. Batista secured more than 800,000 votes to Grau's 575,000.

The Batista presidency (1940–44) had several salutary effects. Most immediately, it ended the anomalous situation whereby effective political power
was transferred from constitutional civil authority to the army chief of
staff. The 1940 election served to reinvest the constitutional office of the
presidency with the power and prestige that had accrued to Batista personally. The demands on Batista the president were no longer the same as the
demands on Batista the army chief. He had acquired a larger constituency
and accumulated debts to the political coalition that had carried him into
office. Batista now presided over the return of patronage and political
appointment to the presidential palace. In early 1941 custom-houses, long
a source of military graft, were transferred to the Ministry of the Treasury.
Army-sponsored education projects passed under the authority of the Ministry of Education. Supervision over lighthouses, maritime police, merchant marine and the postal system returned to appropriate government
ministries.

These developments came as a rude jolt to the old *septembrista* command, long accustomed to the exercise of more or less unchecked authority. Many officers viewed the Batista presidency with great expectation, as
a logical conclusion to a decade of army pre-eminence. The transfer of
army perquisites to civil authority, therefore, quickly aroused the ire of
the senior *septembrista* officers and military confidence in Batista declined.
Friction between Camp Columbia and the presidential palace increased,
and in early 1941 erupted into a short-lived revolt of senior officers. The
collapse of the army plot raised presidential authority to a new high.
Scores of *septembrista* officers was retired; others received new assignments
abroad. A year later the size of the army was reduced and budget alloca-
tions cut. By the end of his term, Batista had restored constitutional
balance of power and re-established civilian control over the armed forces.

Batista had also the good fortune of serving as a wartime president.
Cuba's entry into the war in December 1941 served to facilitate trade
agreements and loan and credit programs with the United States. The
decline of sugar production in war-torn Asia and Europe spurred Cuban
producers. Between 1940 and 1944 the Cuban crop increased from 2.7
million tons to 4.2 million tons, the largest harvest since 1930. The
value of Cuban raw sugar production for the same period also increased,
from 110 million pesos to 251 million pesos. Cuba was also the benefi-
ciary of several important trade deals with the United States. In 1941
both countries signed a lend-lease agreement whereby Cuba received
arms shipments in exchange for U.S. use of Cuban military facilities. In

the same year, the United States agreed to purchase the full 1942 sugar crop at 2.65 cents per pound. A second agreement similarly disposed of the 1943 crop. With the continued revival of sugar production, the economy moved out of a state of lethargy, public works programmes expanded and prosperity returned.

The war was not an unmixed blessing. Prices increased and shortages of all kinds became commonplace. The lack of shipping and risks of transporting goods across the Atlantic severely restricted Cuban trade with Europe. Cuban cigar-manufacturers lost the luxury markets of Europe, and no amount of increase in the export of tobacco leaf to the United States could compensate for this. Tourism registered a marked decrease, the number of travellers falling from 127,000 in 1940 to 12,000 in 1943. As a result, there was sufficient dissatisfaction to generate a lively political debate in 1944, when presidential elections was scheduled. The government candidate, Carlos Saladrigas, campaigned with the active support of Batista. He was opposed by Ramón Grau San Martín in a spirited campaign with Saladrigas extolling the Batista administration and Grau recalling nostalgically his one hundred days of power in 1933. Indeed, the mystique of Grau as well as the appeal of the Auténticos was primarily derived from those heady and exalted days of 1933. In 1944, Grau promised more of the same, and an expectant electorate responded. In the June poll Grau obtained more than one million votes, sweeping five out of six provinces, losing only Pinar del Río. After more than a decade of unsuccessful bids for political power, Grau San Martín and the Auténticos had finally won a presidential election.

The Auténtico victory raised enormous popular expectations in the reform program that had served as both the legacy and promise of the PRC. However, neither the Grau government (1944–48) nor his successor Carlos Prío Socarrás (1948–52) was able to meet Cuban expectations. The Auténticos had spent the better part of their political lives as victims of persecution, imprisonment and forced exile. From the earliest political stirrings against Machado in the 1920s, through the revolutionary tumult of the 1930s and the disappointing electoral set-backs of the early 1940s, the first republican-born generation had been banished to a political wilderness. Their debut in Cuban politics had been as inglorious as it was impoverishing. By the mid-1940s, idealism had given way to cynicism, and public office no longer offered the opportunity for collective improvement as much as it provided the occasion for individual enrichment. Government fell under a siege of new hungry office-seekers, and their appetite was voracious. For the first time, Auténticos acquired control over the disposal of lucrative posts and privileges. Embezzlement, graft, corruption and malfeasance of public office permeated every branch of national, provincial and municipal government. Political competition became a fierce struggle to win positions of wealth. Politics passed under the control of party thugs, and a new word entered the Cuban political lexicon: *gangsterismo*. Violence and terror became extensions of party politics and the hallmark of Auténtico rule.

The number of persons on the government payroll more than doubled in size, from 60,000 in 1943 to 131,000 in 1949. By 1950, some 186,000 persons, 11 per cent of the work force, occupied active public positions at national, provincial and municipal levels of government; another 30,000 retired employees were on the state payrolls. An estimated 80 per cent of the 1950 budget was used to pay the salaries of public officials. Pensions accounted for another 8 per cent of national expenditures. The Auténticos responded to their electoral success with considerable uncertainty, fearful that their tenure would be brief and their rule temporary. These circumstances served to distinguish PRC corruption from the practices of its predecessor, emphasis being given to immediate returns and spectacular graft. Grau was accused of having embezzled $174 million. The outgoing Minister of Education in 1948 was believed to have stolen $20 million. The Minister of Finance in the Prío government was accused of misappropriating millions of old bank notes scheduled for destruction.

That these conditions prevailed, and indeed so permeated the institutional fabric of the republic during the Auténtico years, was in no small way a result of the post-war prosperity enjoyed by the Cuban economy. The economies of sugar-cane producers in Asia and beet-growers in Europe were in ruin. During World War II world sugar production declined by almost 60 per cent, from a combined cane and beet production of 28.6 million tons in 1940 to 18.1 million tons, and it was not until 1950 that world production overtook pre-war levels. As world production fell and prices rose the opportunities for Cuban producers were palpable. This boom never quite reached the proportions of the 'dance of the millions' following the First World War, but it certainly produced a level of prosperity not known since those years. Between 1943 and 1948, Cuban sugar production increased almost 50 per cent, from 2.8 million tons to 5.8 million tons. By 1948, sugar had come to constitute a high of 90 per cent of the island's total export value.

Good times came to Cuba in dramatic form. Sugar exports accounted for a nearly 40 per cent increase in national income between 1939 and 1947. Record sugar exports and simultaneous import scarcities caused by the war produced a large balance-of-payments surplus, averaging more than $120 million annually between 1943 and 1947. Domestic industrial and commercial activity increased over the decade while government revenues from taxation rose from $75.7 million in fiscal year 1937–8 to $244.3 million in 1949–50. Food prices increased almost threefold between 1939 and 1948 and the cost of living rose more than twofold. Inflation would have been more acute if it had not been for the wartime import scarcities and the willingness of many individuals and institutions to keep the better part of the savings in idle balances. The money supply increased 500 per cent between 1939 and 1950 while the cost of living rose only 145 per cent. Over roughly the same period the dollar, gold and silver holdings of the national treasury rose from $25 million to $402 million; the net balance abroad from $6 million to more than $200 million; and the public's dollar holding from $14 million to $205 million.

Post-war economic opportunities were squandered not only by corruption and graft but also by mismanagement and miscalculation. Few structural changes were made in the economy, the chronic problems of unemployment–under-employment and a weak agrarian order remaining unaltered. The economy began to decline by the late 1940s, and only a temporary reprieve provided by a rise in the price of sugar occasioned by the Korean War delayed the inevitable crisis. The problem of inflation increased and capital generated by the post-war prosperity war either invested abroad or mismanaged at home. 'Much of the savings of Cubans', the International Bank for Reconstruction and Development reported of these years, 'has gone abroad, been hoarded or used for real estate construction and for speculation'.[9] Between 1946 and 1952 the Cuban gross fixed investment as a percentage of gross income was only 9.3 per cent (in Argentina it reached 18.7 per cent, in Brazil 15.7 per cent and in Mexico 13.4 per cent).

Of course, these developments were not entirely new. They had long been associated with the boom-or-bust mentality of the Cuban sugar economy. But in the late 1940s and early 1950s such conditions had far-reaching implications. The fact that sugar continued to dominate the Cuban economy persuaded potential investors to retain large portions of

[9] International Bank of Reconstruction and Development, *Report on Cuba* (Baltimore, 1951), p. 7.

their assets in liquid form. It contributed to fostering the desire for quick profits and it discouraged new investments and economic diversification. Cuba continued to depend upon an export product in which competition was especially intense, the decline of rival producers as a result of the war engendering a false sense of security. In fact, the economy was not growing fast enough to accommodate the estimated annual 25,000 new jobs required to meet the growing numbers of people entering the labour market. These problems would have challenged even the most enlightened administration. They were historical and structural, and defied easy solution. The Auténticos, however, were far from enlightened. These were years that began with great hope and ended with disappointment and disillusionment.

At the same time, conditions were generally difficult for the Communist Party, now renamed the Partido Socialista Popular (PSP). Collaboration with Batista had gained the party access to the cabinet, and in the 1944 elections the PSP obtained three seats in the Senate and ten in the lower house. By the 1948 elections the party could claim some 160,000 supporters. But PSP fortunes declined markedly during the Auténtico years. The Cold War undermined PSP influence, and the Auténticos lost no opportunity to expand their power. They moved against the Communist-controlled trade unions and by the late 1940s had established PRC control over key labour organizations. The government confiscated the PSP radio station and continually harassed the party newpaper. But even as PSP influence declined, the party remained an effective political force.

The apparent indifference with which the PRC leadership viewed the historical mandate of 1933 and the electoral triumph of 1944 created dissent and tension within the party. By 1947, PRC misgovernment resulted in an open rupture when Eduardo Chibás, a prominent student leader in 1933, broke with the Auténticos and organized the Partido del Pueblo Cubano (Ortodoxo). In claiming to uphold the ideals of the 1930s, the Ortodoxos became generally associated in the popular imagination with economic independence, political freedom, social justice and public honesty. Perhaps the most gifted orator of the era, Chibás articulated public grievances and crystallized popular discontent against the incumbent Auténticos in a campaign that thrived on spectacular accusations and disclosures of high level government corruption. Chibás contributed powerfully to a final discrediting of the Auténtico administration, undermining what little remained of public confidence in government leadership. However, Chibás' suicide in 1951 produced instead mass disillusionment, resignation and indifference despite the fact that the Prío government remained substantially weaker after its three-year bout with the fallen Ortodoxo leader. Thoroughly disgraced, politically weak, morally bankrupt, the Auténticos presided over a discredited government and a demoralized body politic.

Batista would later derive enormous satisfaction in recounting the details of his return to power in 1952. Within one hour and seventeen minutes, he boasted, the military conspirators overturned the Auténtico government. And, indeed, the *cuartelazo* of 10 March unquestionably owed much of its success to the organizational prowess of its planners. At 2:40 A.M. the rebels seized all the capital's principal army posts, from which military units moved into the city to garrison strategic positions. Bus and rail stations, airports, docks, electricity plants, radio transmitters, banks and offices of government ministries passed into army control. Later that morning city residents awoke amid rumours of a coup and turning to radio broadcasts heard only uninterrupted music. Telecommunication service to the interior was interrupted. Sites of potential protest demonstrations against the coup passed under military control. The university and opposition press offices were closed. Local headquarters of various unions and the Communist Party were occupied, and leading activists arrested. Constitutional guarantees were suspended.

The ease with which Batista and the army executed the plot and consolidated power, however, reflected considerably more than adroit application of conspiratorial talents. The effects of nearly a decade of graft, corruption and scandal at all levels of civilian government had more than adequately paved the way for the return of military rule in 1952. The *cuartelazo* simply delivered the coup de grâce to a moribund regime. Indeed, general indifference to the coup underscored the depth of national cynicism with politics. The discredited Autfentico government possessed neither the popular confidence nor the moral credibility to justify an appeal for popular support; its overthrow simply did not warrant public outrage. On the contrary, for many the coup was a long-overdue change. To business and commerce Batista pledged order, stability and labour tranquillity. To the United States he promised respect for foreign capital. To political parties he promised new elections in 1954.

The Auténtico and Ortodoxo parties proved incapable of responding effectively to Batista's seizure of power. The Ortodoxos were leaderless and the Auténticos could not lead. After 1952 Cuba's two principal parties became irrelevant to a solution of the political crisis. In much the same way that the crisis of the 1930s had brought about the downfall of the traditional parties, events in the 1950s contributed to the demise of the Auténticos and Ortodoxos. Both parties, to be sure, duly condemned the violation of the 1940 Constitution, but neither party responded to the army usurpation with either a comprehensive program or compelling plan of action. The little opposition that did arise originated largely outside the organized political parties, principally from ousted military officers, splinter political groups and personalistic factions of the major parties. Once again, however, a new generation of Cubans responded to the summons and filled the political vacuum.

The early challenges to the *batistato* failed, and failed without much fanfare. An abortive plot, the routine arrest of café conspirators, the quiet retirement of dissident army officers, were not the stuff to arouse the national conscience or inspire national resistance. The attack on Moncada barracks in Santiago de Cuba led by Fidel Castro in July 1953 also failed, but it was the dimension of its failure that distinguished it from its ill-starred predecessors: the plan was as daring as its failure was spectacular. It served to catapult Castro into contention for leadership over the anti-Batista forces and elevated armed struggle as the principal means of opposition in the mid-1950s.

The much anticipated elections of 1954 offended all but the most cynical *batistianos*. The major political parties in the end refused to participate and the leading opposition candidate withdrew. Running unopposed, obtaining a majority of the mere 40 per cent of the electorate that voted, Batista won a new term of office. After 1954 those moderate political forces that had counted on elections to settle national tensions found themselves isolated and without alternatives. One last effort to negotiate a political settlement of the deepening crisis occurred in 1955 when representatives of the moderate opposition arranged a series of conferences with Batista. The Civic Dialogue, as the discussions became known, sought to secure from the President the promise of new elections with guarantees for all participants. He refused. The stage was now set for armed confrontation.

The first response was not long in coming. Late in 1955 student demonstrations resulted in armed clashes with the army and police, and the repression which followed persuaded student leaders of the necessity to organize a clandestine revolutionary movement, the Directorio Revolucionario. A year later, an insurgent group of Auténticos took up arms and attacked the Goicuría army barracks in Matanzas. In 1957, after an unsuccessful assassination attempt against Batista, the Directorio Revolucionario also turned to rural insurgency and organized a guerrilla front in Las Villas province known as the II Frente Nacional del Escambray. It was, however, in the Sierra Maestra mountains of Oriente province that the fate of the Batista regime was being determined.

Within three years of the attack on Moncada, Fidel Castro had organized another uprising in Santiago timed with his return from Mexico aboard the small yacht *Granma,* but the revolt of 30 November 1956 was crushed well before the *Granma* crew set foot on Cuban soil. Moreover, alerted to the arrival of the expeditionaries, government forces overwhelmed the landing party at Alegría de Pío in southern Oriente, reducing the force of some eighty men to a band of eighteen. Having failed in a dramatic bid for power, deprived of arms, ammunition and supplies, the *Granma* survivors sought refuge in the southeastern mountain range.

The character of the guerrilla campaign which followed conformed to the geopolitical setting of the Sierra Maestra. Castro and his men commenced operations in a peripheral region of the island where the politico-military presence of the government they were committed to overthrowing amounted to no more than isolated Rural Guard outposts. In waging war against the Rural Guard, however, the rebels attacked both the local power-base of the Batista regime and the symbolic expression of Havana's presence in the Sierra Maestra region. For decades, Rural Guard commanders arbitrarily terrorized rural communities. Hence, however modest rebel successes against the rural constabulary may have seemed, they did pose a serious challenge to Havana's politico-military authority in Oriente province.

The group of *Granma* survivors attracted early recruits from the mountain population, and with this slightly augmented force the insurgents mounted their early offensives. By January 1957, the rebel force was sufficiently strong to overpower the Rural Guard post at La Plata; in a second action in May 1957 the guerrillas defeated the Rural Guard station at El Uvero. News of insurgent victories kept Cubans alive to the struggle unfolding in the Sierra Maestra and attracted new recruits to the guerrilla camp. Rebel operations also forced government forces to leave the security of the cities to give chase to the rural insurgents. In the process the arbitrary manner in which the government conducted field operations served further to alienate the rural population and generate additional support for the guerrilla force.

Insurgent victories forced the government to concede enclaves of liberated territory throughout Oriente. Throughout 1957 and early 1958 the size of the rebel army increased and field operations expanded. By mid-1958, a fifty-man column under Raúl Castro had established the Second Front in northeastern Cuba, consolidating several rebel bands operating in the region. A column of some thirty-five men under Juan Almeida subsequently opened another front in the area around Santiago de Cuba and likewise succeeded in consolidating and augmenting insurgent forces. In April 1958, Camilo Cienfuegos left the Sierra stronghold with a small patrol of eight or ten men. Still another column under Ernesto Che Guevara operated east of Turquino peak.

The expanding struggle in the countryside was accompanied by growing resistance in the cities. Urban underground groups, most notably the Civic Resistance movement, coordinated acts of sabotage and terror in Cuba's principal cities. As kidnappings and assassinations increased the regime responded with increasing ferocity, which served to increase its isolation.

Anti-government opposition was not confined to civilian political groups. By the mid-1950s dissension had become rife within the armed forces. Batista's return to power had signalled the wholesale transformation of the army command, old *septembrista* officers, many of whom had retired in the previous years of Auténtico rule, returning to positions of command. Political credentials and nepotism governed promotions and commands in the early 1950s, Batista virtually dismantling the professional officer corps. The return of *septembrista* officers produced widespread demoralization among younger commanders who were proud of their academy training and took umbrage at appointments that made a mockery of professional standards and placed the old sergeants in positions of command.

In April 1956 the first of a series of army conspiracies jolted the government. The plot led by Colonel Ramón Barquín implicated more than two hundred officers, including the most distinguished field commanders of the army. In the subsequent reorganization some four thousand officers and men were removed, reassigned and retired. In September 1957 another conspiracy resulted in a mutiny at the Cienfuegos naval station that was part of a larger plot involving the principal naval installations across the island. In the same year conspiracies were uncovered in the air force, the army medical corps and the national police. By the late 1950s, then, Batista was facing both mounting popular opposition and

armed resistance with an army that was increasingly politically uncertain
and professionally unreliable.

The Cuban crisis during the 1950s went far beyond a conflict between
Batista and his political opponents. Many participants in the anti-Batista
struggle certainly defined the conflict principally in political terms, a
struggle in which the central issues turned wholly on the elimination of
the iniquitous Batista and the restoration of the Constitution of 1940. But
discontent during the decade was as much a function of socio-economic
frustration as it was the result of political grievances. By the 1950s sugar
had ceased to be a source of economic growth and lacked the capacity to
sustain continued economic development. Yet all sectors of the Cuban
economy remained vulnerable to the effects of price fluctuations in the
international sugar market. The decline in sugar prices between 1952 and
1954 precipitated the first in a series of recessions in the Cuban economy
in the course of the decade. At the same time the effects of the reciprocity
treaty of 1934 had taken their toll, impeding in Cuba the industrial
development characteristic of other Latin American countries during the
post-war period. Such local industry which did exist had to face strong
foreign competition with little or no tariff protection and there was little
incentive to expand manufactures beyond light consumer goods, largely
food and textiles. With the Cuban population expanding at an annual rate
of 2.5 per cent, and 50,000 young men alone reaching working age every
year, only 8,000 new jobs were created in industry between 1955 and
1958.

Investment patterns were at once a cause and effect of these conditions.
Investment in industry did not keep up with the availability of domestic
savings. At the same time considerable sums of capital were transferred
abroad, principally in the form of profits on foreign investments in Cuba
and through Cuban investments outside the island. Few Cubans invested
in government securities or long-term stocks, preferring liquidity, principally in short-term funds in banks abroad or safety-deposit boxes at home.
The few long-term investments made were principally in U.S. stocks. By
1955 investment in real estate exceeded $150 million, most of it in
southern Florida. In contrast, U.S. capital controlled 90 per cent of the
telephone and electricity services in Cuba, 50 per cent of railroads and 40
per cent of sugar production. Cuban branches of U.S. banks held 25 per
cent of all bank deposits. Indeed direct U.S. investment in Cuba, which
had declined during the depression, expanded steadily after the Second

World War, reaching a peak of \$1 billion (\$386 million in services, \$270 million in petroleum and mining, \$265 million in agriculture and \$80 million in manufacturing) in 1958.

Not only did labour's share of net income decline during the 1950s – for example, from 70.5 per cent of 66.4 per cent between 1953 and 1954 – but unemployment and under-employment increased. By 1957, the best year during the middle 1950s, 17 per cent of the labour force was generally classified as unemployed, while another 13 per cent had been reduced to under-employment. In the sugar industry, one of the principal sources of employment for Cuban labour – it employed an estimated 475,000 workers, approximately 25 per cent of the labour force – some 60 per cent of the workers were employed for six months or less, with only 30 per cent employed for more than ten months. The average sugar-worker was employed for less than one hundred days of the year. As unemployment increased so, too, did resistance to measures raising productivity. Sugar-workers successfully opposed mechanized cutting and bulk loading, cigar-workers were able to limit mechanization and dock-workers put up fierce resistance to it. Successive labour laws through the 1940s and 1950s all but made the dismissal of workers impossible and job security became an issue of paramount importance. One result of all this was to reduce further the ability of Cuban exports to compete successfully in international markets.

Significant distinctions existed within the Cuban labour force. Agricultural workers typically earned less than 80 pesos a month, which compared unfavourably with an average industrial wage of approximately 120 pesos a month plus pension allowances and other fringe benefits, particularly if a worker was employed by a major company or belonged to a strong union organization. Moreover, rural Cuba enjoyed few of the amenities and services that had come to characterize life in the island's cities. On the contrary, the one-third of the population which lived in the countryside suffered abject poverty and persistent neglect. Only 15 per cent of rural inhabitants possessed running water as compared with 80 per cent of the urban population. Only 9 per cent of rural homes enjoyed electricity as compared with 83 per cent of the urban population. Medical and dental personnel as well as hospitals and clinics tended to concentrate in the cities while a combination of poverty and isolation served to exclude the countryside from virtually all access to educational services. The national illiteracy rate of 20 per cent concealed that of 40 per cent in the countryside while in Oriente province it was more than 50 per cent. The peasantry lived at the margins of society and outside the body politic. Nor were these conditions likely to change soon. Vast areas of rural Cuba were held in latifundia farms. Twenty-two large sugar companies operated one-fifth of the agricultural land, much of this in reserve for the prospective periodic boom that planters so eagerly awaited. Cattle ranches also accounted for vast acreage, from which large numbers of peasants were excluded as either workers or owners.

By the mid-1950s even the Cuban urban middle class felt itself in crisis. To be sure, Cuba enjoyed one of the highest per capita incomes in Latin America ($374), ranked in 1957 second after Venezuela ($857). Only Mexico and Brazil exceeded Cuba in the number of radios and televisions per one thousand inhabitants. The country ranked first in telephones, newspapers, and passenger motor vehicles. Daily average food consumption was surpassed only by Argentina and Uruguay. Consumption of foreign imports, principally U.S. products, increased from $515 million in 1950 to $649 million in 1956 and $777 million in 1958. Middle-class Cubans, however, found little personal comfort in statistical tallies that touted their high level of material consumption and placed the island near the top of the scale of per capita incomes in Latin America. The United States, not Latin America, was the Cuban frame of reference. Cubans participated directly in and depended entirely on the United States economic system in much the same fashion as U.S. citizens, but without access to U.S. social service programmes and at employment and wages levels substantially lower than their North American counterparts. The Cuban per capita income of $374 paled against the United States per capita of $2,000, or even that of Mississippi, the poorest state, at $1,000. (And in 1956 Havana ranked among the world's most expensive cities – fourth after Caracas, Ankara and Manila.) This disparity was the source of much frustration, particularly as middle-class Cubans perceived their standard of living fall behind the income advances in the United States. Per capita income in Cuba actually declined by 18 per cent, for example, during the recession of 1952–4, neutralizing the slow gains enjoyed during the immediate post-war period. In 1958, Cuban per capita income was at about the same level as it had been in 1947. By the late fifties middle-class Cubans, initially deposed to support Batista, were in many ways worse off than they had been in the twenties.

Batista's continued presence in power compounded the growing crisis by creating political conditions that made renewed economic growth impossible. As the International Commission of Jurists later concluded,

administrative dishonesty and political illegality' were in 1958 the most
important obstacles to economic development.[10] Political instability and
conflict were playing havoc with the economy. After the short boom
between 1955 and 1957 tourism was once again in decline, and the
insurgency was halting the flow of dairy, vegetable and meat supplies from
the countryside to the cities. Shortages caused the prices of basic staples to
soar while sabotage and the destruction of property further contributed to
economic dislocation. Sugar production dropped. Indeed, by 1958 the
insurgency had reached its most advanced stage in the three eastern provinces that accounted for more than 80 per cent of the total sugar land and
more than 75 per cent of the annual crop. Shortages of gasoline and oil
brought railroads, trucking and sugar mills to a standstill. It was in 1958
that the 26 of July Movement opened a war against property and production across the island as a means to isolate Batista from the support of
economic elites, both foreign and domestic. The message was clear: conditions of normality would not return until Batista departed. In February
the guerrilla leadership announced its intention to attack sugar mills,
tobacco factories, public utilities, railroads and oil refineries. The destruction of the sugar harvest in particular emerged as the principal goal of
insurgent strategy. 'Either Batista without the *zafra* or the *zafra* without
Batista', the 26 of July intoned again and again. In March the rebel army
command reported having applied a torch to every cane-producing province on the island, destroying an estimated 2 million tons of sugar. As
early as September 1957, the resident *New York Times* correspondent in
Havana cabled that commerce, industry and capital, 'which have whole-
heartedly supported President Batista since he took over the Government
in 1952, are growing impatient with the continued violence in the island'.[11] By 1958, this impatience had turned to exasperation.

Cuba was on the verge of revolution through most of 1958. In July
representatives of the leading opposition groups met in Caracas to organize
a united front and develop a common strategy against Batista. The Pact of
Caracas established Fidel Castro as the principal leader of the anti-Batista
movement and the rebel army as main arm of the revolution. As the
conference in Caracas convened, Batista launched his most formidable
offensive against the guerrillas in the Sierra Maestra. Every branch of the
armed forces participated in the offensive, an estimated 12,000 troops

---

[10] International Commission of Jurists, *Cuba and the Rule of Law* (Geneva, 1962), p. 25.
[11] *New York Times*, September 15, 1957, 4, p. 11.

moving on the Sierra Maestra. Air force squadrons bombed and strafed suspected rebel-held regions while naval off-shore units pounded the south-eastern mountain range. But by the end of the summer the government offensive collapsed, signaling the beginning of the disintegration of the Cuban armed forces. The army simply ceased to fight as desertions and defections reached epidemic proportions. Retreating army units became easy prey for advancing guerrilla columns. Demoralization turned to fear and, ultimately, panic.

The guerrillas launched their counter-offensive in late summer. Within weeks government forces in the eastern half of the island found themselves engulfed by the swelling tide of the armed opposition, isolated from relief and reinforcements as provincial towns and cities fell to guerrilla columns. Local military commands surrendered, often without firing a shot. Loyal troops sought desperately to return west in advance of the revolutionary current that moved inexorably toward Havana from the east.

Two things were now clear; the Batista regime was doomed, and the 26 of July movement under Fidel Castro had established clear hegemony over all the revolutionary factions. In the summer, only months before the fall of the regime, the Communist PSP, which had been proscribed during the second Batista government, had allied itself with the 26 of July Movement. This conversion to Fidelismo won the party several key positions within the 26 of July, most notably within the rebel army columns of Raúl Castro and Ernesto Che Guevara, positions later to serve as the basis of expanding PSP authority in post-revolutionary Cuba.

By 1958, Batista had acquired one more adversary: the United States government. The year began inauspiciously for the Cuban government when, in March, Washington imposed an arms embargo, a move tanta-mount to the withdrawal of support. The suspension of arms shipments contributed to weakening Batista's hold over his supporters, both civil and military, especially since it was declared on the eve of the government's spring offensive. For the better part of the 1950s, Batista had retained army loyalty with assurances that he enjoyed unqualified support from Washington. After March 1958, the army command was no longer sure. According to U.S. ambassador Earl E. T. Smith, intimations that Wash-ington no longer backed Batista, had 'a devastating psychological effect' on the army and was 'the most effective step taken by the Department of State in bringing about the downfall of Batista'.[12]

---

[12] Earl E. T. Smith, *The Fourth Floor* (New York, 1962), pp. 48, 107.

The year 1958 was also an election year, providing Batista with an opportunity to demonstrate to Washington that democratic processes were still capable of functioning, civil war notwithstanding. But to the suprise of few, government candidate Andrés Rivero Agüero triumphed, the electoral hoax further weakening Batista's position both at home and abroad. The victory of the official candidate disillusioned the few who still hoped for a political end to the armed insurrection. Army officers personally loyal to Batista, disheartened by the prospect of a transfer of executive power, lost their enthusiasm to defend a leader already replaced at the polls. Washington rejected outright the rigged presidential succession and announced in advance plans to withhold diplomatic recognition of Rivero Agüero, which undermined political and military support for the regime.

In fact, Washington had already determined to ease Batista out of office. The crisis in 1958 recalled that of 1933 in that the incumbency of an unpopular president threatened to plunge the island into political turmoil and social upheaval. Once again Washington sought to remove the source of Cuban tensions as a means to defuse the revolutionary situation. In early December the State Department dispatched financier William D. Pawley to Havana to undertake a covert mission. The United States, Pawley later recalled, urged Batista 'to capitulate to a caretaker government unfriendly to him, but satisfactory to us, whom we could immediately recognize and give military assistance to in order that Fidel Castro not come to power'. On December 9 Pawley held a three-hour conference with Batista, offering him an opportunity to retire unmolested in Florida with his family. The U.S. envoy informed the President that the United States 'would make an effort to stop Fidel Castro from coming into power as a Communist, but that the caretaker government would be men who were enemies of his, otherwise it would not work anyway, and Fidel Castro would otherwise have to lay down his arms or admit he was a revolutionary fighting against everybody only because he wanted power, not because he was against Batista'.[13] Batista refused.

Even as the United States sought to persuade Batista to leave office, the revolutionary momentum had sealed the fate of the regime. The failure of the government offensive and the success of the guerrilla counter-offensive had a galvanizing effect on Cubans, provoking spontaneous uprisings

---

[13] United States Congress, Senate, *Hearings Before the Subcommittee to Investigate the Administration of the Internal Security Act and Other Internal Laws of the Committee on the Judiciary: Communist Threat to the United States Through the Caribbean*, 86th Cong., 2d Sess. (Washington, D.C., 1959–60), pt. 10, p. 739.

across the island. Large amounts of arms and equipment fell into the control of civilians in the wake of the army retreat, including artillery, tanks and small arms of every type. In the closing weeks of 1958, both the ranks of the urban resistance and the guerrilla columns increased rapidly. By December 1958 the Batistiano army command in Santiago reported that 90 per cent of the population supported guerrilla actions. At about the same time, spontaneous uprisings in Camagüey overwhelmed local army detachments. In the decisive battle of Santa Clara, Guevara's column received decisive assistance from the local population. At the time of the government's summer offensive the guerrillas numbered some 5,000 officers and troops. By January 1959, the rebel army numbered some 50,000.

Batista's expendability was the signal for military intrigue. The army that had ceased to fight in the countryside had become the focal point of political intrigue in the cities. By December no fewer than half a dozen conspiracies were developing in the armed forces. During the early hours of 1 January 1959, as guerrilla columns marched across the plains of central Cuba, General Eulogio Cantillo seized power and appointed Supreme Court Justice Carlos Piedra as provisional president. The 26 of July Movement rejected the coup and demanded unconditional surrender to the rebel army. Pledging to continue the armed struggle, Fidel Castro called for a nationwide general strike.

With the news of Batista's flight, army units throughout the island simply ceased to resist further rebel advances. Cantillo complained to the U.S. embassy that he had inherited the command of a 'dead army'. Seeking to revive the moribund war effort, Cantillo summoned the imprisoned Colonel Ramón Barquín and relinquished to him command of the army. Barquín ordered an immediate cease-fire, saluted the insurgent 'Army of Liberation', and surrendered command of Camp Columbia and La Cabaña military fortress to Ernesto 'Che' Guevara and Camilo Cienfuegos. A week later Fidel Castro arrived in Havana.

4

CUBA SINCE 1959

Fulgencio Batista had been the dominant figure in Cuban national affairs for a quarter of a century. He had ruled Cuba, directly or indirectly, since the military coup of 4 September 1933, except for an interlude of Auténtico rule from 1944 to 1952. He had seemed confident and powerful until the last weeks of his last presidency. But suddenly Batista was gone. On New Year's Eve 1958 he quit, taking with him much of the top echelon of his government. A new leader, young and bearded, who for two years had led a guerrilla war in eastern Cuba, gradually spreading the influence of his forces to the western provinces, slowly assuming the leadership of the urban and the rural resistance to the Batista regime, marched into Havana. Audacious and effective in his military campaign and political skills, persuasive and commanding in his public speech, Fidel Castro had become the leader of the future. Power had passed, somewhat unexpectedly, to a new generation of Cubans.

In January 1959 the old regime collapsed in Cuba and a revolution came to power. The old rules of the game no longer applied and the armed forces that had shaped the life of independent Cuba for so long had crumbled. The rebel army became the defender of the new revolutionary state, sweeping aside the parties that had structured political life in previous decades. Only the Communist party (Partido Socialista Popular, PSP), which had been banned by Batista in the 1950s but reappeared in 1959, was left intact. The fall of the old regime required that new norms, rules and institutions be devised to replace those that had collapsed or been overthrown. The history of Cuba during the next thirty years addressed the needs of revolutionary creativity, the persistent commitment to create order out of revolution, the need to uphold a revolutionary faith in the implementation of that new order.

THE CONSOLIDATION OF REVOLUTIONARY POWER
(1959–62)

Cuba has always been buffeted by the winds of international affairs. Geographically in the heart of the American Mediterranean, it has been coveted by the major powers over the centuries. With the end of four hundred years of Spanish colonial rule and the establishment of United States primacy in 1898, Cuba's link with the United States became the virtually exclusive focus of Cuban internationl relations during the first half of the twentieth century.

In 1959 the U.S. government viewed with concern the affairs of a country that seemed uncharacteristically out of its control. Cuba mattered to the United States because of both its strategic location and its economic importance. The United States operated a naval base at Guantánamo under the terms of a 1903 treaty that recognized nominal Cuban sovereignty but guaranteed the United States the right to operate the base for as long as Washington wished. Despite subsequent Cuban protests, the United States retained the base. While U.S. military forces had not been stationed in Cuba outside Guantánamo for several decades and U.S. government officials had played a reduced role in internal Cuban politics, in the 1950s the U.S. ambassador remained the country's second most important political figure after the President of the Republic. In 1959 the value of U.S. investments in Cuba – in sugar, mining, utilities, banking and manufacturing – exceeded that in every other Latin American country except Venezuela. The United States also took about two-thirds of Cuban exports and supplied about three-quarters of its imports. (And foreign trade accounted for about two-thirds of Cuba's estimated national income.)

Fidel Castro, the 26 of July Movement, which he led, and other revolutionary forces that had participated in the revolutionary war, sought to affirm Cuban nationalism. In the symbols used and histories evoked, in the problems diagnosed and solutions proposed, there was a strong emphasis on enabling Cubans to take charge of their history. There was, however, during the revolutionary war only a limited criticism of U.S. government policies and the activities of U.S. enterprises in Cuba. Castro had bitterly criticized the modest U.S. military assistance initially extended to the Batista government under the formal military agreements between the two countries, but this aid was eventually cut. Castro had also spoken of the expropriation of the U.S.-owned public utilities. However, in the later phases of the guerrilla war, for tactical reasons, Castro seemed to back off from any expropriation proposals.

In the early months of the Revolution there were three principal themes in Cuban-U.S. relations. First, there was mistrust and anger over U.S. criticism of events in Cuba. The Cuban government brought to trial many who had served the Batista government and its armed forces; most of these prisoners were convicted and many were executed. The trials were strongly criticized, in both Cuba and the United States, for observing few procedural safeguards to guarantee the rights of the accused as well as for the severity of many sentences. Fidel Castro and other Cuban government leaders were offended by this, and they denounced their critics in the U.S. mass media (especially the wire services) and the U.S. Congress. The onset of poor relations between Cuba and the United States from January 1959 stemmed from this clash between the values of justice and retribution of revolutionaries and the values of fairness and moderation of a liberal society even toward its enemies.

The second major factor was the Revolution's initial impact on U.S. firms operating in Cuba. The frequency of strikes increased sharply in 1959 as workers sought gains from management under the more favourable political situation. Foreign-owned firms were affected by such strikes and in some cases the question of their expropriation arose. A strike at the Royal Dutch Shell petroleum refinery, for instance, raised the question of the expropriation of British property, authorized by a law issued by the rebels in retaliation for British military sales to the Batista government. Fidel Castro obtained generous concessions from Shell in exchange for forgoing expropriation 'at this time'.[1] Comparable pressures from below affected the revolution in the countryside. The Agrarian Reform Act (issued May 1959), moderate in many respects, was also strongly nationalist. The Instituto Nacional de Reforma Agraria (INRA) was more willing to intervene in labour–management conflicts when farms were foreign-owned, and to suspend the strict application of the law in these cases to expropriate foreign-owned land. Such local agrarian conflicts soured U.S.-Cuban relations.

The third feature of this period was changing Cuban attitudes to new private foreign investment and official foreign aid. On 18 February 1959 Prime Minister Fidel Castro publicly welcomed foreign capital and on 20 March 1959 acknowledged the ample availability of aid. On 2 April 1959

[1] Fidel Castro, *Discursos para la historia* (Havana, 1959), 1: 50–2, 75–81.

the Prime Minister announced that on a forthcoming trip to the United States he would be accompanied by the president of the National Bank and the Ministers of the Treasury and of the Economy to seek funds for Cuba. This trip to the United States in April 1959 became a deadline for making decisions that the overworked revolutionaries had hitherto postponed. Did Cuba's new government want a close relationship with the United States? Was this revolution committed to a Cuba open and profitable for multinational firms? Could its leaders make a genuine and radical revolution with the support of the United Fruit Company, Coca-Cola, the Chase Manhattan Bank or Standard Oil? Would Fidel Castro accept the economic austerity preached by the International Monetary Fund (IMF), embrace U.S. vice-president Richard Nixon, and proclaim U.S.-Cuban friendship at the gates of the Guantánamo naval base? En route to the United States Castro told his economic cabinet that they were not to seek foreign aid from officials of the U.S. government, the World Bank or the IMF, with whom they might speak during their visit. The purpose of the trip, therefore, changed from acquiring aid for capitalist development to gaining time for far-reaching transformations the specific form of which was still uncertain. There is no evidence that the United States, or these international financial institutions, denied aid to Cuba that its government had requested. In fact, Cuba did not ask them for aid. Had such aid been requested and granted, it would have tied Cuba's future closely to the world capitalist economy and to the United States because of the conditions ordinarily attached to such aid in the 1950s. A small number of revolutionary leaders, therefore, concluded well ahead of the rest of the citizenry that it was impossible to conduct a revolution in Cuba without a major confrontation with the United States. A revolution would require the promised extensive agrarian reforms and probably a new, far-reaching state intervention in the public utilities, mining, the sugar industry and possibly other manufacturing sectors. Given the major U.S. investments in these sectors, and United States hostility to statism, revolution at home would inevitably entail confrontation abroad.

The approval of the Agrarian Reform Act was followed in June 1959 by the first major cabinet crisis, which resulted in the departure of the moderates. U.S. ambassador Philip Bonsal presented a formal U.S. government protest on 11 June complaining of irregularities and abuses in the early implementation of the Agrarian Reform Law against U.S. firms. The head of the Air Force, Pedro Luis Díaz Lanz, quit at the end of June and fled to the United States, charging Communist infiltration of the government. President Manuel Urrutia was forced out in July, leaving no doubt that Prime Minister Castro was Cuba's uncontested leader. The question of communism was also an issue for Urrutia, who had stoutly defended the government against charges of communism while accusing the Communists of attempting to subvert the Revolution. Urrutia was replaced by Osvaldo Dorticós (who would serve as president until 1976). The question of communism also mattered for the slowly evolving links with the Soviet Union. The first official contacts with the Soviet Union were made in Cairo by Ernesto 'Che' Guevara in June 1959, although at this stage Soviet–Cuban trade was as insignificant as it had been before the Revolution. Relations with Moscow changed qualitatively from October 1959. And Soviet deputy prime minister Anastas Mikoyan visited Cuba in February 1960 to sign the first important bilateral economic agreement between the two countries and to promote other relations.

U.S.-Cuban relations continued to deteriorate during the second half of 1959. Disputes over Communist influence in the government became frequent and intense. Washington's view of the Cuban government soured as Castro sharpened the vituperative tone of his remarks about the United States. In early March 1960 a Belgian ship *La Coubre,* loaded with arms and ammunition for the Cuban government, exploded in Havana harbor. Prime Minister Castro accused the U.S. government of sabotage. Publicly, the U.S. government protested. Privately, on 17 March 1960, President Dwight Eisenhower authorized the Central Intelligence Agency (CIA) to organize the training of Cuban exiles for a future invasion of Cuba.

The pace of deterioration in U.S.-Cuban relations quickened in the spring and summer of 1960. In late June the Cuban government requested the foreign-owned petroleum refineries to process crude oil it had purchased from the Soviet Union. When the companies refused they were expropriated. At the same time, a newly amended sugar act was making its way through the U.S. Congress. A clause in the bill authorized the President to cut off the Cuban sugar quota; the bill was approved by 3 July. On 5 July, the Cuban Council of Ministers authorized the expropriation of all U.S. property in Cuba. On 6 July, President Eisenhower cancelled Cuba's sugar quota. On 15 July the newly established Bank for Foreign Trade became Cuba's sole foreign-trade agency. On 7 August the expropriation of all large U.S.-owned industrial and agrarian enterprises was carried out, and on 17 September all U.S. banks were confiscated. On 19 October the U.S. government prohibited exports to Cuba except for non-subsidized foodstuffs and medicines. On 24 October, Cuba expropriated all U.S.-owned wholesale and retail trade enterprises and the remaining smaller U.S.-owned industrial and agrarian enterprises. The United States withdrew Ambassador Philip Bonsal on 29 October. U.S.-Cuban diplomatic relations were finally and formally broken in the waning days of the Eisenhower administration in January 1961.

In contrast, Cuban–Soviet relations improved markedly during this period. On 9 July 1960, Prime Minister Nikita Khrushchev declared that Soviet missiles were prepared to defend Cuba 'in a figurative sense'. The first formal military agreement between the two countries was signed within weeks as the Soviet Union pledged to 'use all means at its disposal to prevent an armed United States intervention against Cuba'.[2] This increasing military collaboration between Cuba and the Soviet Union predictably heightened U.S. government hostility towards Havana.

The swift and dramatic changes in U.S.-Cuban relations were paralleled by the reorganization of Cuba's internal political and economic affairs, one consequence of which was a massive emigration to the United States. Washington favoured this emigration through special programs with the aim of discrediting the Cuban government. From 1960 to 1962 net outmigration from Cuba amounted to about 200,000 people, or an unprecedented average of well over 60,000 per year. Most emigrants came from the economic and social elite, the adult males typically being professionals, managers and executives, although they also included many white-collar workers. On the other hand, skilled, semi-skilled and unskilled workers were under-represented relative to their share of the work force, and rural Cuba was virtually absent from this emigration. This upper-middle- and middle-class urban emigration was also disproportionately white. Henceforth, a part of the history of the Cuban people would unfold in the United States. The first wave of emigrants, in part because they could transfer their skills to new workplaces, would experience relative economic and social success over the next thirty years. Politically, they would constitute a strong anti-communist force often sharply at odds with prevailing political opinion among other Spanish-speaking communities in the United States.

In late 1960 and early 1961 the would-be Cuban-Americans were still just Cubans, exiled from their homeland and planning to return. As the United States and Cuban governments came to blows during the second half of 1960, Washington became more interested in assisting the exiles to

---

[2] *Revolución*, 21 July 1960, 1.

overthrow the Castro government. The exiles, however, were deeply divided. Those who were once close to the Batista government were repelled by those who had worked with Fidel Castro during the rebellion or in the early months of his government, although they had broken with Castro over the question of communism and other issues; this antipathy was fully reciprocated. Did Cuba need a restoration or a non-communist transformation? There were many shades of opinion within each side of this fundamental cleavage, personality conflicts further complicating relationships. The U.S. government required a unified Cuban exile leadership if the efforts to overthrow the Castro government with a minimum of U.S. intervention were to succeed.

On 22 March 1961 several key exile leaders agreed to form the Cuban Revolutionary Council presided over by José Miró Cardona, who had been the first prime minister of the Cuban revolutionary government in January and February 1959. Prominent members of the Council included Antonio ('Tony') Varona, former prime minister (and opponent of Batista), as well as Fidel Castro's former Minister of Public Works, Manuel Ray. Manuel Artime, a former lieutenant of the rebel army, was to be the political chief of the invasion force and José Pérez San Román the military commander. Upon the overthrow of the revolutionary regime the Council would become the provisional government of Cuba under the presidency of Miró Cardona. The exiles' Brigade 2506 completed its training in Nicaragua and Guatemala.

The administration of John F. Kennedy inherited the plan for this invasion when it came to office on 20 January 1961. Those who pressed for an invasion used the analogy of covert U.S. support for the overthrow of Guatemalan president Jacobo Arbenz in 1954: effective, at low cost to the United States and with no direct involvement of U.S. troops. Supporters of the invasion argued that it had to proceed soon before Castro's government received enough weapons from the Soviet Union to defeat the challenge. On 3 April the U.S. government published a 'white paper' accusing Castro and his close supporters of betraying what had been an authentic revolution. In the U.S. government's view, Cuba needed a non-communist transformation. President Kennedy agreed to let the CIA-trained invasion force go forward, provided that U.S. forces were not used.

On the morning of 15 April planes piloted by Cuban exiles bombed several airfields in Cuba, creating much panic but little damage. The police responded by imprisoning tens of thousands of suspected dissidents. On Monday morning, 17 April 1961, Brigade 2506 landed at Girón beach on the Bay of Pigs in south-central Cuba. The Cuban government mobilized both its regular armed forces and the militia. Led personally by Fidel Castro, they defeated the invasion force within forty-eight hours and captured 1,180 prisoners. The prisoners were held for trial and interrogation by Castro and others on Cuban national television; they were eventually ransomed for shipments of medical and other supplies from the United States late in 1962. As recriminations began within the Kennedy administration and exile groups in the aftermath of the invasion's failure, Castro triumphantly announced that Cuba's was a consolidated socialist revolution able to defeat its enemies within Cuba as well as the superpower to its north.

If the making of a radical revolution in Cuba required a break with the United States, the defence of a radical revolution in the face of U.S. attack demanded support from the Soviet Union. On 2 December 1961, Fidel Castro proclaimed that he was a Marxist-Leninist and that he would be so until death. In July 1962 Raúl Castro, the armed forces minister, travelled to Moscow to secure additional Soviet military backing. On the Soviet side, the possibility of stationing strategic missiles in Cuba seemed to be a political and military coup. A Soviet strategic base in Cuba would parallel U.S. bases ringing the USSR, and the reaction time and accuracy of a Soviet nuclear attack on the United States would be improved. The 'figurative' missiles of July 1960 became the real missiles of October 1962. The USSR eventually installed forty-two medium-range ballistic missiles in Cuba, and as U.S. intelligence sources gathered information on this President Kennedy was persuaded that the Soviet Union and Cuba sought a major change in the politico-military balance with the United States. On 22 October, Kennedy demanded the withdrawal of Soviet 'offensive missiles' from Cuba and imposed a naval 'quarantine' on the island to prevent the additional shipment of Soviet weaponry. Kennedy also demanded the withdrawal of Soviet L-28 bombers and a commitment not to station Soviet strategic weapons in Cuba in the future.

The world held its breath. Not since the dropping of nuclear bombs on Hiroshima and Nagasaki had nuclear warfare seemed so imminent. Poised on the edge of war, the two superpowers jockeyed over their military relationship. The crisis ended when, without prior consultation with Cuba, the Soviet Union backed down, pulling out all its strategic forces in exchange for the pledge that the United States would not invade Cuba. The United States made that pledge conditional on UN verification of the Soviet withdrawal of strategic weapons, but a furious Fidel Castro refused to allow on-site inspection. In fact, although a formal U.S. pledge to desist from invading Cuba would not be made, an 'understanding' came to govern U.S.-Soviet relations over Cuba. The Soviet Union was not to deploy strategic weapons in Cuba nor to use it as a base of operations for nuclear weapons. The United States, in turn, would not seek to overthrow Castro's government. Thus the Cuban missile crisis was a major victory for the U.S. government, since it publicly humiliated the Soviet government over the central question of the day, and yet it also sealed the end of U.S. influence in Cuba. Both Fidel Castro and his exile opponents lost the total support of their superpower allies, but the former would eventually recognize the he had gained much more because his rule was saved by the wisdom of Soviet actions.

As peace returned to the Cuban countryside at the beginning of 1959, the economy began to recover. The revolutionary government sought to stimulate economic growth and, at the same time, to pursue its redistributive goals by altering the structure of demand. The real wages of non-agricultural workers rose sharply, and urban rents for lower-rent dwellings were slashed by as much as 50 per cent. Early in 1959, the government seized all property that had belonged to former president Batista and to his close associates. For the first time in Cuban history the state acquired a major role owning and directly operating productive activities. Unlike most other major Latin American countries, Cuba had not developed an entrepreneurial state sector of the economy before 1959; consequently, there was very little experience about how it might be operated. These problems were to be compounded after 1960 when many managers were dismissed, emigrated or were arrested.

The experiment with a mixed economy was brief because, as we have seen, the Cuban government socialized most of the means of production during its confrontation with the United States. That confrontation need not have affected Cuban-owned business, but on 13 October 1960, 382 locally owned firms, including all the sugar mills, banks, large industries, and the largest wholesale and retail enterprises, were socialized. Three days later the Urban Reform Act socialized all commercially owned real estate. The 1959 Agrarian Reform Act had destroyed Cuban-owned as well as foreign-owned latifundia although it still permitted small- and medium-sized private farms. Because many Cuban entrepreneurs had close connections with the United States and were presumed to oppose the revolutionary government, the survival of revolutionary rule seemed to require that management and ownership pass to loyal revolutionaries, however technically incompetent they might be. These actions also reflected a self-conscious decision to socialize the economy even though the Revolution's socialist character would not be proclaimed officially until April 1961. Such decisions were justified on the grounds of national security and also because direct ownership and control over the means of production were deemed necessary for economic planning. Economic centralization was viewed as a rational step to generate economic growth. The revolutionary leaders were not compelled to socialize the economy: they acted autonomously and, in their view, prudently to implement an ideological vision of the society they wished to build. Power had to be concentrated in the hands of the few to achieve the aspirations of the many: that was at the heart of the evolving ideology.

The turning-point in internal Cuban politics occurred in October and November 1959, months before the break with the United States, or the first treaties with the Soviet Union. On 15 October, Raúl Castro, Fidel's younger brother, became defence minister (a title changed later to Minister of the Armed Forces), a post he held thereafter. Raúl Castro had had a distinguished military career. He was primarily responsible for the organization and development of the Cuban armed forces and their eventual victories at the Bay of Pigs and in overseas wars, the military being the one undoubtedly effective organization created in the first thirty years of revolutionary rule. He also assumed the post of second-in-command to his older brother in all affairs of state, civilian as well as military, playing an important role in the revitalization of both party and government in the 1970s. Raúl was Fidel's formally designated successor in case of death, with the power to enforce the succession.

On 18 October 1959, Rolando Cubelas – the 'unity' candidate with Communist support – defeated Pedro Boitel, the candidate of the 26 of July Movement at the university, in the elections for the presidency of the Federación Estudiantil Universitaria (FEU) after intervention by Fidel Castro, and aligned the FEU with the shift toward Marxism–Leninism. (In 1966, Cubelas would be arrested for plotting to assassinate Fidel Castro, for which it seems he had the support of the U.S. Central Intelligence Agency.)

On 19 October, Huber Matos, military commander of Camagüey province and one of the leading figures of the revolutionary war, resigned along with fourteen officers over the rising influence of communism in the regime. When Matos was arrested the entire 26 of July Movement executive committee in Camagüey province resigned and its leader was detained. Matos spent two decades in prison; his courageous resistance in jail and his unwillingness to collaborate or to bend to the will of his captors became a symbol of strength to the opposition.

In November the Confederación de Trabajadores Cubanos (CTC) held its tenth congress to select a new leadership. The 26 of July Movement's slate had a clear majority. The government pressed for 'unity' with the Communists, but the congress delegates refused and when Fidel Castro addressed the congress his words were interrupted by the chanting of 'twenty-six, twenty-six'. He attacked those who would use that label 'to stab the revolution in the heart'.[3] He argued that the revolution's defence required avoiding partisan quarrels; he asked for and received authority from the congress to form a labour leadership. He picked the 'unity' slate, including the communists.

At the end of November most of the remaining moderates or liberals in the Council of Ministers, including Minister of Public Works Manuel Ray and National Bank president Felipe Pazos were forced out of office. Of the twenty-one ministers appointed in January 1959, twelve had resigned or had been ousted by the end of the year. Four more would go out in 1960 as the revolution moved toward a Marxist-Leninist political system. The elimination of many non-communists and anti-communists from the original coalition, along with the regime's clash with business, were the internal ingredients of the transformation of the revolution's politics. A new leadership consolidated centralized and authoritarian rule. But among those in the new government coalition, only the old communists had the political and administrative experience to make the new system work.

As internal and international conflicts deepened during 1960 and 1961 the government developed its organizational apparatus. Having obtained control over the FEU and the CTC, the leadership established a militia with tens of thousands of members to build support and to intimidate internal enemies. The Federación de Mujeres Cubanas (FMC) was also founded in August 1960 and the Comités de Defensa de la Revolución (CDR), which eventually encompassed millions of members, were established in September 1960. Committees were set up on every city block, in each large building, factory or work centre (eventually, CDRs would be dismantled in

[3] *Revolución*, 23 November 1959, 4.

work centres so as not to duplicate the work of the labour unions) in order to identify enemies of the Revolution for the state's internal security apparatus. Gossip became an arm of state power. The Asociación de Juventud Revolucionaria (AJR) was launched in October 1960, merging the youth wings of the old Communist Party, the Revolutionary Directorate, and the 26 of July Movement. A few years later the AJR became the Unión de Jóvenes Comunistas (UJC), the youth affiliate of the Communist Party. The Asociación Nacional de Agricultores Pequeños (ANAP) was founded in May 1961; it excluded the medium-sized farm owners (whose property would be expropriated in 1963) and sought to cut across the divisions that existed between producers of various commodities.

A new Communist party was founded in the summer 1961. Called the Organizaciones Revolucionarias Integradas (ORI), it was created through the merger of three pre-existing organizations: the 26 of July Movement, the Revolutionary Directorate, and the old Communist Party, the PSP. The first two of these had by this stage become phantom organizations: the Revolutionary Directorate had been deprived of much independent power after January 1959, while the battles for control over the university students' federation and the labour unions had crippled the 26 of July Movement's capacity for independent political activity. PSP members brought several advantages to the ORI. They were bridge-builders between the rest of the leadership and the Soviet Union. They had some theoretical knowledge of Marxism–Leninism, in contrast to the rest of ORI, and they had long experience of party politics as well as the organization of mass movements. The PSP had run the CTC during its first decade and party militants were the only ORI members with prior government experience, having served in Congress in pre-revolutionary years and contributed ministers (including Carlos Rafael Rodríguez) to Batista's war cabinet in the early 1940s. As a result, they initially dominated the ORI.

The organization of party cells, selection of party members, and all promotions and dismissals had to be cleared through the office of the powerful Organization Secretary, veteran PSP leader Aníbal Escalante. Party cells asserted their authority over administrators, and a preliminary system of political commissars was introduced in the armed forces. Membership in the party, moreover, emphasized recruiting those who had belonged to the older political organizations; recruitment of genuine newcomers was not encouraged. Escalante gave preference to his old PSP comrades, who knew best how to organize a party and were personally loyal to him. This proved unacceptable for old 26 of July members and especially to the military commanders of the guerrilla war. In March 1962, Fidel Castro denounced Escalante for 'sectarianism', removed him from the job as organization secretary, and exiled him to Czechoslovakia. A massive restructuring of the ORI followed; about half the ORI members were expelled, many of them from the PSP faction. New efforts were made to recruit members not only from the pre-existing organizations but also from among those who had been too young for political activity before 1959. The scope of party authority in the armed forces was drastically limited; henceforth, military commanders would have supreme military and political authority within the armed forces. In 1963 the ORI's name was changed to the Partido Unido de la Revolución Socialista (PURS).

In 1962, revolutionary power had become consolidated, although the leaders would not realize this for some years. The threat from the United States began to recede as a consequence of the settlement of the missile crisis. Fidel Castro had established his mastery of Cuban politics and his pre-eminence over all rivals. The organization of revolutionary rule beyond his charisma was under way, even though it would become effective only in the 1970s. Opponents of the regime took up in arms in every province in the first half of the 1960s, being especially strong in the Escambray mountain region of Las Villas province. Thousands of Cubans died in this renewed civil war (1960–6), the rebels including the peasantry of southern Matanzas province as well as those whose social and economic interests were more obviously at stake. They were, however, thoroughly defeated by 1966. (With many like-minded Cubans emigrating, the regime, in effect, exported the opposition.) The main task had become the management of the economy, the rapid decline of which imperilled the accomplishment of other government goals.

ECONOMIC POLICIES AND PERFORMANCE

Following the establishment of a command economy under conditions of political crisis, early economic policy in revolutionary Cuba sought development through rapid industrialization. Cuba's overwhelming dependence on the sugar industry was seen as a sign of under-development. As Che Guevara, Minister of Industries and architect of the strategy, put it, 'there can be no vanguard country that has not developed its industry. Industry is the future'.[4]

---

[4] *Obra revolucionaria* 10 (1964): 14.

Central state ministries were established and a development plan was formulated with help from many sources but especially from the Soviet Union and East European countries. Cuba was utterly unprepared, however, for a centrally planned economy. It lacked technical personnel (now in the United States or prison) as much as statistics. The plan for 1962 and the plan for 1962–5 were both fantasies. Data did not exist to formulate them and knowledge of economic management was primitive. The plans called for the achievement of spectacular growth targets. Instead, the Cuban economy collapsed in 1962. The government froze prices and imposed rationing for most consumer products. The ration card, a fixture in Cuban life ever since, combines two important aspects of the government's economic performance: relative failure to generate economic growth coupled with relative success in protecting the needs of the poorest Cubans and reducing inequalities in access to basic goods and services. Redistribution policies sought not only to enhance the purchasing power of the poor but also to curtail that of the rich. Wage scales set maximum as well as minimum salaries. In a suprising move the government changed the currency overnight; those who did not have their funds in state banks could not exchange old for new pesos. Their savings were worthless.

The Cuban economy fell further in 1963. Sugar production was down by over a third of its 1961 level as a result of the government's drastic policies to diversify away from the crop. Production elsewhere in agriculture and industry also suffered. Imports of machinery and equipment for accelerated industrialization, coupled with the decline of revenues from sugar exports, created a balance-of-payments crisis. In June 1963, Prime Minister Castro announced a new strategy which once again emphasized sugar production and slowed down the efforts toward industrialization. The strategy of sugar-led development was reaffirmed in 1964 when the Soviet Union and Cuba signed their first long-term agreement that guaranteed better, stable bilateral sugar prices and, eventually, Soviet subsidies above world market prices for Cuban sugar.

The government's strategy called for increasing sugar production until 10 million tons of raw sugar would be produced in 1970. This policy was opposed by a number of technicians and administrators in the sugar industry, but they were overruled. The 1970 sugar production target became a point of pride, a demonstration that Cubans could take charge of their history against all odds. Just as the impossible dream had been achieved in the late 1950s when Batista was overthrown, so would another be achieved at the end of the 1960s as committed revolutionaries demonstrated that they could raise the level of sugar production from 3.8 million tons in 1963 to 10 million tons in 1970. The doubters would be proven wrong again.

The new strategy was complicated, however, by a top-level debate on the nature of socialist economic organization. One side, led by Minister of Industries Che Guevara, argued that the part of the economy owned by the state was a single unit. Money, prices and credit should operate only in dealing with Cuban consumers or foreign countries. The market law of supply and demand could and ought to be eliminated to move rapidly toward communism. Central planning was the key. All enterprises would be branches of central ministries. All financing would occur through the central budget by means of non-repayable interest-free grants. All enterprise deficits would be covered by the state. Buying and selling among state enterprises would be simple accounting transactions. Money would be a unit of accounting but would not be used to assess profitability. Material incentives (wage differentials, bonuses, overtime payments) to labour would be phased out. The central government would allocate resources by planning physical output and would set all prices needed for accounting.

The other side argued that the part of the Cuban economy owned by the state was not a single economic unit but a variety of enterprises independently owned and operated by the state. Transfers from one enterprise to another did involve buying and selling, with profound implications for the allocation of resources. Money and credits were needed to maintain effective controls over production and to evaluate economic performance. Enterprises had to meet their own production costs and not simply be bailed out for their deficits by the central bank; they had to generate their own funds for further investment, maintenance and innovation. Material incentives to labour were essential to maintain productivity and quality and to reduce costs. If the first model required extraordinary centralization, the second required more economic autonomy for each firm.

The debate was eventually resolved when Che Guevara left the Ministry of Industries in 1965 (to be engaged in revolutionary campaigns in Africa and in South America until his death in late 1967) and the ministry was divided into its former sub-components. Some of Guevara's political allies in other ministries lost their jobs. However, Guevara's policies were generally adopted, and their implementation was carried out to extremes. Much of the calamity in economic performance in the late 1960s is due to Guevara's flawed vision as well as to the administrative chaos unleashed by

Fidel Castro and his associates, as Castro himself would recognize in a dramatic speech on 26 July 1970 when the Cuban economy lay in ruins.

The radical model required the fuller centralization of the economy. As early as 1963 a second Agrarian Reform law was issued to expropriate the middle-sized farms of the rural bourgeoisie that had remained after the implementation of the 1959 law. By the end of 1963, the state owned 70 per cent of all land, and only small farms remained in the private sector. The climax of collectivization came with the 'revolutionary offensive' of the spring 1968 when consumer service shops, restaurants and bars, repair outfits, handicraft shops, street food outlets and even street vendors passed to state ownership and management. Except in a limited way in a small part of the agricultural sector, no economically productive activity could take place in the late 1960s without going through a government agency. It was the time of the state as hot-dog vendor, ice-cream parlour, barber and radio repairman. Although an illegal black market developed, for vegetables as well as for plumbing services, the government had put the economy in a strait jacket.

Paradoxically, as the economy became thoroughly centralized, the means for central planning and control were abandoned. In the late 1960s there were neither real year-to-year national plans nor any medium-term planning. From late 1966 onwards only sectoral planning occurred, but on a limited basis and with little effort to reconcile the often conflicting claims on the same resources from unconnected enterprises and projects. A central budget was also abandoned, not to reappear until a decade later. Fidel Castro launched an attack on 'bureaucratism' which crippled the capacity of several central agencies. Financial accounting and auditing were discontinued; statistics were kept only in physical quantities (e.g., pairs of shoes). It became impossible to determine the costs of production for most items.

The changes in labour policy were equally dramatic. The phasing out of material incentives was to be coupled with a renewed emphasis on moral incentives: the revolutionary consciousness of the people would guarantee increased productivity and quality and reductions in cost. Workers would be paid the same regardless of variations in effort or quality. Those who worked overtime would be expected to do so voluntarily and would not receive extra pay. Money was seen as a source of capitalist corruption. This change in policy occurred in the wake of a major structural change in the labour market. Whereas Cuba had suffered a persistently high rate of overt unemployment before the Revolution, this had been reduced quickly in the early 1960s and been transformed into a labour shortage. Many of the formerly unemployed had been put to work in state enterprises. Productivity per worker plummeted as employment rose and production declined. Inefficiency and under-employment were institutionalized in the new economic structures. And yet this was also an extraordinary human achievement; it allowed most able-bodied Cubans the dignity of some work and the commitment to use their talents in a constructive way.

Economic performance was complicated by another change in the structure of the labour market. Because of the highly seasonal nature of the all-important sugar industry, pre-revolutionary employment patterns had suffered sharp seasonal oscillations. Workers worked very hard when they were employed to save for the expected unemployment during the 'dead season'. When the revolutionary government guaranteed employment (or sufficient unemployment compensation) throughout the year to all able to work the pre-revolutionary structural incentive to work hard weakened. Thus the revolutionary government succeeded in eliminating a perpetual source of misery – the fear of destitution as a worker stimulus – but this was not replaced by new effective incentives for high-quality work. As material incentives were removed on top of these structural changes, the problem of low and declining worker productivity worsened, as did labour shortages. No moral exhortations were incentive enough.

Since moral incentives proved insufficient to stimulate production and productivity the government engaged in mass mobilization for work in the sugar fields and other sectors of the economy. These so-called volunteers – who often lacked the right to refuse – were deployed throughout the country rather ineffectively. They were supplemented by a substantial portion of the personnel of the Cuban armed forces. Having defeated the internal counter-revolution by 1966, the armed forces committed themselves to directly productive economic activities including the harvesting of sugar cane. Military officers became harvest supervisors as the desperate effort to produce 10 million tons of sugar in 1970 combined with the shift towards radical economic policies and reliance on revolutionary consciousness. A new revolutionary citizen was to have emerged to lead Cuba to economic emancipation.

The economy was recorded as having produced 8.5 million tons in 1970 (by juggling the artificially low 1969 figures): the highest in Cuban history but still 15 per cent below target. Between 1968 and 1970 the Cuban economy was badly dislocated as resources were shifted among sectors without regard to the cost of achieving the impossible dream, the central government's actions promoting chaos while labour was coerced to work under military discipline without adequate rewards. Production in cattle-raising and forestry declined from 1968 to 1970, as did over 68 per cent of all agricultural product lines and over 71 per cent of all industrial product lines; even the fishing sector, the best performer under revolutionary rule, showed more declines than increases.

By 1970 Cuba's economic growth performance was dismal. Two sharp recessions had marked the beginning and end of the decade, the intervening years showing only a modest recovery. The standard of living was extremely spartan, and discontent surfaced at all levels. To his credit, Prime Minister Castro took personal responsibility for the disaster and changed economic policies in the first half of the 1970s.

Relief for the Cuban economy came from an unexpected quarter: the world sugar market. Prices for sugar in the free world market soared from an annual average of 3.68 cents of a dollar in 1970 to 29.60 cents in 1974. Given that sugar exports had continued to account for about four-fifths of all exports, this price bonanza alone accounts for much of Cuba's economic recovery in the first half of the 1970s. The government also moved to reform internal economic organization by adopting and adapting the Soviet economic model. Central macro-economic planning reappeared in the early 1970s, enabling Cuba to adopt its first five-year plan in 1975. The first plan (1976–80) proved too optimistic and many of its targets were not reached (the growth rate was one-third below plan) since it had been based on the assumption that world sugar prices would remain higher than proved to be the case in the late 1970s. Nonetheless, it was more realistic than anything the government had adopted before. A central budget was again designed and implemented from 1977. Financial accounting and auditing were reinstituted, and material incentives received renewed emphasis as various reforms in monetary, price and wage policies sought to align supply and demand more accurately. The Soviet Union also channelled considerable resources to bring the Cuban economy afloat again.

One indication of how badly organized the Cuban economy had been in the 1960s is that many of the new measures formulated early in the 1970s could not be implemented until the late 1970s or early 1980s. Delays were also caused, however, by some opposition to the liberalization of the Cuban economy. And yet, as the 1980s opened, farmers were allowed to sell the surplus to their state quotas in markets where prices were unregulated and transactions were between private persons; this also occurred in handicraft markets and in the after-hours and weekend contracting of services. At long last one could hire a plumber or buy tomatoes without dealing with a bureaucracy. State enterprises received greater autonomy to contract labour directly rather than depending wholly on the central labour agency. A new management system was gradually adopted and implemented in the late 1970s and early 1980s to provide managers with more autonomy and authority. It allowed each enterprise to retain some profits to distribute to managers and workers at the end of the year and to improve the enterprise and working conditions. Wage differentials, over-time pay and bonuses came to play a major role in labour incentives. Higher wages were paid for better-quality work, productivity improve-ments, cost reduction and longer hours.

The economy prospered almost spectacularly during the first half of the 1970s, Cuba's growth rate in those years comparing well with that of the world's leading growth performers. However, the economy stagnated dur-ing the second half of the decade except for 1978. The third major severe recession under revolutionary rule was under way by mid-1979, encourag-ing the outburst of emigration in 1980 just as the prolonged recession of the late 1960s increased the emigration of those years.

Weak economic performance at the beginning of the 1980s put pres-sure on the country's foreign-debt service payments. Although Cuba has not been a major borrower in the international capital markets, its hard-currency foreign debt in 1982 was about $3 billion. When foreign trade became more concentrated with the Soviet Union exports generated less revenue for servicing the hard-currency debt. The ensuing negotiations with European, Arab and Japanese bankers led to policies that decreased consumption levels in the early 1980s in order to meet Cuban debt obligations.

One major difference between these two periods of economic perfor-mance was the price of sugar. Although it rose steadily from 1970 to 1974, it fell to an average of about 8 cents per pound during the second half of the 1970s. After a short-lived rise in late 1980 and early 1981 the world price of sugar fell to the 6- to 8-cent level. Moreover, troubled by its own weak economic performance, the Soviet Union in 1981 cut by one-sixth the price it paid for Cuban sugar while continuing to raise the prices it charged for its exports to Cuba. Cuba's terms of trade with the Soviet Union in 1982 – when Cuba had to reschedule its debts with market-economy lenders – were one-third lower than in 1975. The recov-ery of the price the Soviets paid for Cuban sugar in subsequent years prevented a more severe economic crisis, even if the Cuban–Soviet terms of trade remained well below what they were in the mid- to late 1970s. Sugar prices remained closely related to the swings in Cuban economic performance, underscoring the commodity's persistently central role in the economy.

The adoption of some economic reforms in the early 1970s had quick and positive results, but by the late 1970s productivity improvements were more difficult to attain. Fidel Castro told the third party Congress in 1986 that Cuba still suffered from 'the absence of comprehensive national planning for economic development'. He added that the new management system, after a good beginning, had 'no consistent follow-through to improve it. The initiative was lost and the creativity needed to adapt this system to our own conditions – a system largely taken from other countries – never materialized'. Even 'the budget continued to be ineffective. Rather than regulating spending, it, in effect, promoted it'.[5]

To address these problems, in April 1986 Castro launched a process that he called 'rectification'. Cuba was the only communist regime in the late 1980s to back off from market mechanisms in order to improve production and efficiency. Castro denounced heads of state enterprises for having become apprentice capitalists. He lashed out at the lure of 'vile money'. To stamp out the curse of the market, in May 1986 the government banned the farmers' markets that had been legalized in 1980. Other anti-market measures were adopted and Castro lashed out against the reliance on bonuses to motivate the workers, calling once again for moral incentives to build a better society. The fact that the economy fell into a recession in 1986–7 partly reflected the inefficacy of these measures to rid Cuba from the vestiges of capitalism. There was, however, another enduring problem. The second half of the 1970s was also the period of the two major African wars and of the deployment of large numbers of Cubans overseas, which relied on the mobilization of reservists. A majority of Cuban troops in Ethiopia, about four-fifths of the Cuban troops in Angola and almost all Cuban personnel in Grenada were reservists at the peak of the wars and the U.S. invasion. Given the desire to win the wars and to perform well overseas in military roles, some of the best managers, technicians and workers were taken from the home economy for the overseas army, contributing to a decline in productivity and efficiency in various sectors since the

[5] *Granma Weekly Review*, 16 February 1986, special supplement, 6, 7.

late 1970s. Although the number of Cuban troops in Ethiopia was reduced sharply by the mid-1980s, more than 50,000 Cuban troops remained in Angola until the war ended in 1988.

The Cuban revolutionary government sought to generate economic growth from the moment it arrived in power but except for the recovery of the early 1970s these policies did not succeed. There was no growth at all during the 1960s. The economy's performance after 1975 failed to reach many planned targets. It generated only modest real economic growth and suffered a major recession as well as serious international debt problems. The structure of production diversified only a little. Sugar remained king, generating about four-fifths of export revenue. However, the government had also implemented a strategy of import substituting industrialization, evolving gradually in the 1970s and continuing in the 1980s – decades after such strategies appeared in most major Latin American countries. Cuba's factories now provided a wider array of light- and medium-industry products. However, their inefficiency and the poor quality of their products remained a problem while non-sugar agricultural production continued to perform poorly with few exceptions (eggs, citrus fruits). Cuba was unable to diversify its international economic relations to any great extent: there was overwhelming dependence on one product (sugar cane) and one country (the Soviet Union). The tendency in the late 1970s and 1980s was to retain dependence on both.

On the other hand, government economic performance was impressive with respect to redistribution. There was a strong and generally successful commitment to provide full employment for all able-bodied citizens (despite the reappearance of overt unemployment in the 1970s, reaching 5.4 per cent in 1979), even at the cost of under-employment and inefficiency. Equally, access to basic goods at low prices was provided through the rationing system, even at the cost of subsidizing consumption. The government's policies in the 1960s dramatically reduced inequalities between social classes and between town and country. The improvement in the rural poor's standard of living was outstanding. The trend in the 1970s and early 1980s toward greater use of material incentives led to a new inequality that stimulated good managerial and worker performance. Nevertheless, the leadership retained its commitment to meet the basic needs of its people, and Cuba remained a very egalitarian society by Latin American standards.

SOCIAL TRENDS

Cuba underwent a demographic transformation after the Revolution came to power. There was a 'baby boom' in the early 1960s, the crude birth-rate increasing by about a third compared to the late 1950s; then the crude birth-rate stayed above 30 births per 1,000 population from 1960 to 1968. The principal explanation for the baby boom is probably the improved economic conditions for lower-income Cubans resulting from redistributional policies and improved health facilities in the rural areas. Increased wages, an end to overt unemployment, reduced rents and guaranteed access to basic necessities, including education and health care, provided a 'floor' for all Cubans. At the same time, the government launched a campaign to promote marriages, including the legalization of the many pre-existing consensual unions. Contraceptive supplies, previously available from the United States, were cut off by the U.S. trade embargo. The emigration broke up families and opened up new opportunities for relationships for those remaining in Cuba. The emigration of doctors and other health-care personnel reduced opportunities for abortion, as did the more effective enforcement of a pre-revolutionary law restricting abortion.

The initial impact of the baby boom was masked by emigration. Population growth rates declined in the early 1960s, but when the first wave of emigration was shut off at the time of the missile crisis the growth rate reached the highest level since the 1920s: over 2.6 per cent per year. The baby boom also began to have a dramatic impact on the primary school system, which had to expand overnight, and on the delivery of other social services to the young. The government's ability to deliver such services is a striking demonstration of its commitment to support the young even in years of economic decline.

The baby boom was followed by a baby bust. The crude birth rate was reduced by half between the end of the 1960s and the end of the 1970s, when the population growth rate was one-third of what it had been in the mid-1960s. As a result of the emigration outburst, there was a net decline in population in 1980, when Cuba's age pyramid showed that the population aged fifteen to nineteen (the peak of the baby boom) was 50 per cent larger than the population aged twenty to twenty-four (born just before the Revolution). One consequence of the baby boom was to allow the government regularly to station 35,000 young men in its overseas armed forces. The population under age five (the 'baby bust') was somewhat smaller than the population aged twenty to twenty-four, and it was one-third smaller than the population aged fifteen to nineteen. The baby bust had as many implications for social services as did the baby boom; one initial effect was Cuba's ability to export primary school teachers to work overseas in foreign-aid missions. In the long run, the baby bust might have made it more difficult for Cuba to station its armies overseas in the 1990s.

Cuban fertility had been declining gradually before the Revolution. The high level of social modernization probably contributed to the renewed fertility decline, but its magnitude and suddenness in the 1970s could not be explained with reference to long-term processes alone. The new fertility decline began in the late 1960s with the economy's sharp deterioration. However, it continued unabated during both the economic recovery of the first half of the 1970s and the economic slow-down at the end of the decade. The economy's poor performance is a necessary but insufficient condition for explaining the fertility decline. In 1964, restrictions on abortion were eased. Abortion became legal and easy, Cuba's abortion ratio (the number of abortions per 1,000 pregnancies) rising steadily from the 1960s so that by the end of the 1970s two out of five pregnancies were ended by abortion. Only Bulgaria, Japan and the Soviet Union had a higher abortion ratio. Indeed, abortion probably became the main birth-control method. While the number of abortions doubled from 1968 to 1978, the number of live births fell by two-fifths. Other means of contraception, however, also became more available within the national health system and these contributed to a fertility decline too. After the sharp increases of the previous decade the marriage rate stabilized in the mid- and late-1970s, but the divorce rate quadrupled from its pre-revolutionary level, about one in three marriages ending in divorce throughout the 1970s. It is likely that the greater incidence of divorce helped to reduce the birth rate. The continuing severe housing shortage also discouraged marriages because couples did not wish to live with their in-laws, or if they did, there was rarely space to house children. The permanent stationing of some 50,000 Cubans overseas in the late 1970s must also have contributed to reduce fertility.

According to the 1981 national census, there were 9,706,369 Cubans living in Cuba, one-fifth of whom lived in the city of Havana – a slightly smaller proportion than in the 1970 census. Cuba had become an urban country. While the level of urbanization increased slowly between 1953 and 1970 (from 57 per cent to 60 per cent), it jumped to 69 per cent in 1981. Urban growth also occurred outside the capital. While Havana grew 7.7 per cent from 1970 to 1981, Victoria de las Tunas grew by 58 per cent and Holguín and Bayamo by more than 40 per cent. Seven other cities grew by more than 24 per cent in that period, and the number of towns with a population of 95,000 or more doubled in the 1970s. In short, urbanization occurred mostly outside the primate city (Havana), a rare outcome by Latin American standards.

The experience of women changed considerably under revolutionary rule. As we have seen, women were more likely to get married, get divorced and have an abortion. They were much more likely to have children during the 1960s than during the 1970s. The proportion of women in the labour force also doubled from the late 1950s to the late 1970s, when they accounted for 30 per cent of the labour force. This resulted, however, from a gradual increase rather than from an abrupt change brought about by the Revolution. The increased entry of women into the labour force reflected an evolving social modernization although some government policies may have helped it. By contrast, the participation of Cuban women who emigrated to the United States increased much more and much more quickly: proportionately, twice as many Cuban-origin women in the United States than in Cuba were employed in the labour force in 1970, when a majority of Cuban-American women but only a quarter of Cuban women were in the labour force.

   Some Cuban government policies discouraged female incorporation into the labour force. The government reserved certain categories of jobs for men on the grounds that women's health would be impaired were women to be engaged in those occupations, although no evidence was released to justify that policy. As the young 'baby boom' workers entered the labour force rapidly, government policies sought to maintain a constant sex ratio in the labour force instead of helping the proportionate incorporation of women.

   There was an impressive increase in the numbers of women throughout the educational system. Women were represented at levels comparable to their share of the population in formerly predominantly male professional schools at the university, such as medicine, the natural sciences and economics. Although they remained under-represented in engineering and agronomy and over-represented in primary and secondary school teaching and in the humanities, a fundamental shift had occurred. The government, however, imposed quotas to limit the increase in women's enrolment in certain professional schools such as medicine on the grounds that women were more likely to interrupt their careers and that women doctors would be less suitable for service in the armed forces.

Women's participation in politics lagged considerably. Women accounted for only 13 per cent of the Central Committees of the Communist Party of Cuba chosen in 1980 and 1986; there were no women in the party Secretariat and no women in the top government organ, the Executive Committee of the Council of Ministers. The first woman entered the party's Political Bureau in 1986: Vilma Espín, Raúl Castro's wife and president of the Women's Federation. Women were also under-represented at the middle ranks of leadership. Surveys suggested the persistence of sexual stereotypes in the home (despite government efforts through a Family Code approved in the mid-1970s to equalize status between spouses in the family), the workplace and in politics. Women and men clung to traditional female roles.

There was little research on race relations after the Revolution. Because Cuba's black and mulatto population was disproportionately poor, and because the poor benefited disproportionately from government policies, blacks were likely to have benefited from such policies. Available surveys suggested stronger black than white support for the government; until 1980 blacks were greatly under-represented among Cuban exiles. The 1980 emigration outburst included urban blacks in numbers comparable to their share of the urban population. The government eliminated the few racially discriminatory legal bars that existed before the revolution but this had modest impact. The government sought to include the symbolism of Cuba's African heritage at the forefront of the justifications for Cuba's actions in African countries. However, the gaps between whites and blacks may not have changed as much during the past decades. For example, although health standards for the entire population improved, the relatively higher vulnerability of blacks to diseases (especially parasitic diseases that afflict poor populations) continued. The gap in access to health care between whites and blacks did not change much either, despite the undoubted gains in this regard for most Cubans.

Perhaps because the leaders of the revolutionary movement in the 1950s were disproportionately white and because they continued to command the heights of power, blacks were greatly under-represented in the top organs of government and party. The level of black representation changed little from before the revolution – when Batista was Cuba's first mulatto president – to the 1986 party congress when President Castro declared it a matter of party policy to increase the black share of top party organs; whereas one-third of the total population was black (1981 census), the black share of the 1986 Central Committee was just one-fifth. Only in elections to local municipal assemblies were blacks apparently represented in numbers comparable to their share of the population.

Since the government claimed to have solved racial problems, it became subversive to argue that they persisted even if in modified form. The government banned associations of black intellectuals and politicians that had existed before the Revolution. A number of those who insisted there were still serious racial problems in Cuban society, or distinctive intellectual issues among Afro-Cubans, became exiles.

Cuba's educational transformation was the revolutionary government's most impressive achievement. The government advanced Cuba's social modernization by the sharp reduction of illiteracy (down to 12.9 per cent in the 1970 census and to 5.6 per cent in 1979), starting with a major campaign in 1961 which was continued through the extensive adult education system. The government expropriated all private (including Church-affiliated) schools. After difficulties during the 1960s, the government accomplished virtual universal attendance at primary schools. Average educational levels in the labour force jumped from bare literacy in the 1964 labour census to sixth grade in the 1974 labour census and to eighth grade in the large 1979 demographic survey. In 1979, two-fifths of the adult population had completed the ninth grade and two-thirds the sixth grade.

The boom in primary education reflected both government conscious policy and the need to accommodate the baby boom. By the late 1970s, primary school enrolments had begun to decline as a result of the baby bust. From 1974–5 (the peak year in primary school enrolment) to 1980–1, primary school enrolment (including preschool) fell 20 per cent. The remarkably adaptive school system increased junior high school enrolment by 121 per cent and senior high school enrolment by 427 per cent over the same period. Between 400,000 and 700,000 people per year were enroled in adult education schools during the 1970s.

The primary school system reduced – but did not eliminate – the differences in access to quality education between urban and rural Cuba. A generous programme of scholarships also helped to reduce class differences in access to education at the post-primary levels. There were a number of serious problems of quality in Cuban schools during the 1960s – high drop-out rates, low levels of teacher training, poor student and poor teacher performance in the classroom. Although some of these problems remained, the qualitative improvement in the 1970s matched the still excellent quantitative performance inherited from the 1960s. Many people deserved credit for these accomplishments, including Fidel Castro, whose concern with education was a key feature of the government's commitment. However, the long-serving vice-president of the Council of Ministers and Minister of Education, José Ramón Fernández, deserved special mention. He skilfully managed the transition from the baby boom to the bust, the adjustments and expansions of enrolment, and the marked improvements in the quality of education, notwithstanding the problems, that, as he recognized, still remained.

Higher education had a more tortuous history. Enrolment declined in the 1960s, to increase only in the next decade. Faculty ranks were decimated by politically inspired dismissals and emigration. Most students were enroled only in night school, where the quality of the instruction and the experience ranged from poor to variable because many teachers were overworked, resources were limited and there were too many students. There was a strong technical bias to higher education that encouraged enrolment in engineering and discouraged it in the humanities. The academic study of the social sciences was neglected, and that which was undertaken avoided contemporary issues of political significance within Cuba. Since 1959, however, there had been superb historiographical scholarship whose crowning glory was Manuel Moreno Fraginals's trilogy on the sugar mill in the eighteenth and nineteenth centuries (*El ingenio*). Good historiography stops generally around 1935, just before the beginning of the subsequently embarrassing alliance between Batista and the Communist Party.

The universities were organized on a broad 'industrial model', to train professional personnel in a hierarchical system. They de-emphasized the development of the liberal arts or the possibility of active intellectual criticism of major political, social, economic or cultural problems. Many of Cuba's leading writers of the 1960s and 1970s lived overseas (Guillermo Cabrera Infante, Severo Sarduy, Reinaldo Arenas, Heberto Padilla, Edmundo Desnoes, Antonio Benítez Rojo, among others) or had died (Alejo Carpentier and José Lezama Lima). Political criteria were among the factors in making decisions on student admissions even to non-political professions such as medicine and despite the fact that the universities and the Academy of Sciences emphasized applied technical research. Medical research, and research on the agriculture and processing of sugar cane, both with long pre-revolutionary traditions, were the major areas of scientific achievement.

Although Cuba had a high level of literacy (about three-quarters of all adults) and relatively high levels of school enrolment before the Revolution, these had stagnated in the middle third of the twentieth century. The revolutionary government thus took up the task of educational modernization where it had been left in the 1920s to institutionalize an educational revolution that was rightly the pride of its people and government and an outstanding example of sustained commitment to other countries. Cuban schoolteachers ably served their country's foreign policy and the needs of ordinary students over three continents. The educational system, however, was inhospitable to political and intellectual dissent; it restricted freedom of expression and repressed many critics. The fruits of education and culture were thus curtailed. For this tragic loss, Cuba served as a negative example of the uses of government power to limit the full development of human potential.

Government policies and performance in the area of health care also registered appreciable success. The government quickly established health care as the right of every citizen, expanding the system of free provision that had existed before the Revolution. There were early advances in the rural areas, improving the delivery of health care and narrowing the gap between town and country. However, general performance deteriorated during the 1960s compared to the quite highly developed pre-revolutionary health system, this trend largely resulting from the worsening health care in the cities, where most people lived. Many doctors and other health-care professionals left the country and because they had been concentrated in Havana the capital suffered disproportionately. Existing medical services and facilities were disrupted by political and military mobilizations. Inefficient production of medicines and the disruption of ties with the United States led to a shortage of medical supplies which had a particular impact on upper-income urban consumers with access to and resources to buy imported medicines. The emergency health-care training program to replace the departing exiles was uneven in quality, and the health system was affected as much as other areas of state enterprise by the disorganization of the 1960s.

During the early 1960s the general as well as the infant mortality rates worsened. The infant mortality rate (deaths under age one per 1,000 live births) rose from thirty-five in 1959 to forty-seven ten years later, the rates for major diseases also worsening during these years. The commitment of government budgetary resources to urban health care faltered as resources were channelled to the rural areas. Indeed, until the early 1970s the performance of the health-care system was not unlike that of the Cuban economy: much better in redistribution among social classes and geographic regions than in growth. By the mid 1970s, thanks in part to preceding economic improvements, the system made great advances. The infant mortality rate fell to 18.5 per 1,000 by the time of the 1981 census, and morbidity rates fell across the spectrum of serious diseases. It must be remembered, however, that Cuba already had a rather mature health-care system on the eve of the Revolution. Thus, six of the top eight causes of death were identical in 1958 and in 1981; heart disease, cancers, diseases of the central nervous system, influenza and pneumonia, accidents and early childhood diseases. On the other hand, although acute diarrheic diseases, homicides, tuberculosis and nephritis were among the top ten causes in 1958, they had been replaced by suicides, diabetes, congenital malformations and respiratory diseases by 1981. These changes brought Cuba closer to the typical health profile for an industrial country in ways that could have been predicted from Cuba's long-term pattern of health-care modernization.

At the start of the 1980s the government's most significant accomplishment in health care remained the reduction of inequality in access to health care among social classes and regions. Havana's advantage over eastern Cuba narrowed. The set-backs of the 1960s were overcome and health standards genuinely improved, building on the good but insufficient levels of the 1950s. Cuba posted talented health-care personnel in three-dozen countries the world over. Some of these programmes sold their medical services to host governments, earning foreign exchange for Cuba's transnational state enterprises. Most such programmes, however, were free of charge to the recipient country.

The revolutionary government's poor performance in housing construction resulted from insufficient production, inefficiency and disorganization in the construction and construction-materials industries. The government did not give high priority in the allocation of construction resources to meeting the housing needs of the population. Its principal goals in this area included the building of hospitals, schools and military installations and the deployment of some of the best construction teams overseas.

In the late 1940s and early 1950s, with a population half of that three decades later, pre-revolutionary Cuba built almost 27,000 housing units per year. In the early 1960s, the rate fell to just over 17,000 units per year; very little housing was built in the radical period of the late 1960s. During the first Five Year Plan (1976–80), just over 16,000 housing units per year were built. The trend in the late 1970s was towards a decline in the rate of housing construction at the same time as more construction workers were deployed overseas and the Cuban armed forces expanded: Cuba built almost 21,000 housing units in 1973 (the peak year since 1959) but not even 15,000 in 1980.

The housing situation was alleviated somewhat by the emigration. From 1959 to 1975, emigration made available about 9,300 units on the average per year; during those same years, average housing construction was about 11,800 units. This meant that about one-third of the new demand for housing went unsatisfied each year. Considering that much of the pre-revolutionary housing stock was already in deplorable condition and that there was much evidence that thousands of housing units collapsed out of poor maintenance, Cuba faced a terrible housing problem in the 1980s. The housing shortage and the resultant overcrowding have been among the major causes for Cuba's high divorce rate and rapidly declining fertility rate.

POLITICS AND GOVERNMENT

The central figure in Cuba's revolutionary politics was Fidel Castro, his leadership remaining charismatic in the sense that it depended on the conviction that he did not depend on election by his followers but had been 'elected' by a supernatural authority or some 'historical force'. He also depended on the citizenry's sharing that conviction. Castro's sense of mission was a persistent theme in his many public statements. The concluding phrase to the edited version of his defence at his trial for attacking the Moncada barracks on 26 July 1953 provided the first major statement of this belief: 'Condemn me; it does not matter to me. History will absolve me'.[6] History-as-god elects the revolutionary leader to act with and for his followers. Or, as he put it in perhaps the most difficult speech of his government career when he reported publicly on the economic collapse of

---

[6] English text in Rolando Bonachea and Nelson P. Valdés (eds.), *Revolutionary Struggle. 1947–1958: The Selected Works of Fidel Castro* (Cambridge, Mass., 1972), vol. 1.

the late 1960s: 'If we have an atom of value, that atom of value will be through our service to an idea, a cause, linked to the people'.[7] The cause, the idea, history incarnate, elects the leader to rule. Castro's sway over his associates and many ordinary citizens has been the single most striking political fact of contemporary Cuban history.

Castro's political style emphasized active engagement as opposed to theoretical pursuits. It also highlighted the power of self-discipline and conscious action, as opposed to the pre-revolutionary Communists who were waiting for objective conditions to ripen to launch their revolution when Castro's forces swept into power and in contrast to those economists who argued that the strategy to produce 10 million tons of sugar in 1970 was madness. Subjective will was the fundamental resource for revolutionary leaders to overcome objective obstacles in war, politics or economics. A vanguard, an elite, must lead the people and awaken them to their historical responsibilities. Moreover, only the maximum possible effort toward the optimal goal was worth pursuing. The apparently unattainable goal was alone worthy because it was clear that the revolutionary consciousness of women and men provided the essential margin for victory. An activist, determined vanguard would reach for the future – and conquer it.

This approach to politics brought the Cuban Revolution to power and led the revolutionary government to undertake a number of successful activities, ranging from victory in the battlefields of the Horn of Africa to the overcoming of illiteracy. It also led to some disasters and tragedies, of which the economic and social experiments of the late 1960s provide the best general example. But many other smaller projects were also disasters, responding to a whim or a passing thought of Castro's to which subordinates dedicated themselves with fervour and commitment for no sensible purpose. This style of leadership bred intolerance toward critics, dissenters, or even those who were just somewhat unconventional. This style of rule rejected out of hand the hypothesis that the great leader's policies might be in error – until disaster struck.

Revolutionary rule was legitimized not only by charisma but also by performance. Cuba, its new leaders said from the moment they seized power in 1959, had been delivered from a terroristic, corrupt, abusive and illegitimate political system. Fidel Castro's consummate oratorical skills – alternately mellow and fierce, jocular or insulting towards his enemies,

[7] *Granma Weekly Review*. 2 August 1970, 6.

thoughtful or emotional, learned and complex before professional audiences or simple, funny and tender in dialogue with schoolchildren – became one of the Revolution's most powerful weapons. He commanded the airwaves of radio and television in a country where both were well established by 1959. He moved incessantly throughout the country as a revolutionary prophet touching, moving, educating and steeling his people for combat: to struggle for a new life, a better future, against known and unknown enemies.

The government continually emphasized its redistribution to the benefit of lower-income people, and especially the better-implemented policies in education and health care. Even when government leaders acknowledged the failure of economic growth strategies, they stressed the gains accomplished in redistribution and social services. A social cleavage, much clearer than at any other point in Cuban history, became the basis for majority support for revolutionary rule in the difficult days of the early 1960s. Nationalism was a further source of legitimacy, affirming the cultural, political and historical integrity of the Cuban nation and emphasizing the unity of the people rather than the legitimacy which might have been derived from any one segment such as the proletariat. Nationalism gained further strength from the struggle against the U.S. government. The class enemies became 'worms'; the foreign enemies 'imperialists'.

In the absence of national elections from 1959 to 1976, or of other effective organizational channels to voice grievances and opinions, charisma, political deliverance, redistribution and nationalism were the pillars on which the right to rule was claimed. The Revolution itself, and its maximum leader, were self-legitimating, although this claim was certainly not universally accepted.

The mass organizations taken over in 1959 or created in 1960–1 have since mobilized the population to build political support for the government and to deter internal enemies. While they respond principally to centralized direction, they were by the 1970s exhibiting interest-group tendencies. The ANAP, in particular, was a strong lobbyist in defence of private peasant interests in the early 1960s and again from the mid-1970s to the mid-1980s. It has sought higher prices, easier credits and freer markets for peasants, and it has tried to curtail the forcible expropriation of peasant land by the state. Only in the radical period of the late 1960s was the autonomy of this and the other organizations virtually destroyed. The FEU was dissolved between December 1967 and 1971;

the height of radicalism tolerated none of the autonomy or dissent typical of university students. By the 1970s, however, even the CDRs (Committees for the Defense of the Revolution) had changed. While their
paramount task remained 'revolutionary vigilance', they also adopted
other community self-help missions. The mass organizations participated
in most campaigns, both effective and ineffective, launched by the leadership. Among their most successful tasks were the reduction of illiteracy
and of diseases subject to control through mass immunization campaigns. The CDRs were just as effective in this as they were in political
control. The FMC played a prominent role in the sharp reduction of
prostitution and the re-education and incorporation of former prostitutes
into a new life.

The role of the labour unions in the late 1960s was to support management. Unions were directed to struggle to increase production and productivity, to exceed the goals set in the economic plans, to organize competition ('emulation') among workers to accomplish official aims, and to
reduce costs. Workers were to rise above narrow and temporary interests,
such as better wages and better working conditions, to sacrifice themselves
for the good of the people. Labour was exhorted to heroic efforts and to
respond to moral incentives, voluntary work becoming a euphemism for
unpaid overtime work. In August 1969, President Osvaldo Dorticós denounced the 'abuse of overtime and the deceit of overtime', but his was a
lonely voice and he had little power notwithstanding his title.[8] In 1970
Fidel Castro produced the best epitaph for the unions in this period:
'Unfortunately, for the last two years, our workers' organizations have
taken a back seat – not through the fault of either the workers' organizations or the workers themselves but through our fault, the party's fault,
the fault of the country's political leadership'.[9]

By the second half of 1970 the workers had taken enough. They staged
a general 'strike'. Strikes had been illegal since the early days of the
revolution so the leadership described the 1970 event as 'large-scale absen-
teeism'. Although apparently uncoordinated, some 400,000 workers, a
fifth of the work force, stayed away from work in August and September
1970 on any given day. In Oriente province, the cradle of the revolution, a
majority of agricultural workers were absent from work in August 1970,
and more than a fifth were still staying away in January 1971 even though

[8] 'Discurso del Presidente de la República, Dr. Osvaldo Dorticós Torrado, en la escuela de cuadros de
mando del Ministerio de la Industria Ligera', *Pensamiento crítico* 45 (October 1970): 148.
[9] *Granma Weekly Review*, 4 October 1970, 2.

the new sugar harvest was under way. The elections in local labour unions in autumn 1970 were the freest and most competitive since 1959. Many controls over the election process were lifted. Approximately three-quarters of the local labour leaders elected at that time were new to the job. The changes in policy inaugurated in the first half of the 1970s thus responded, in part, to the 'leading role of the proletariat', forcibly communicating to the government that radical policies were no longer acceptable to labour.

As the conditions of labour improved in the early 1970s so were political controls re-established over the unions. By the time of the Thirteenth Labour Congress in 1973 elections by acclamation (rather than by secret ballot) for unopposed slates had reappeared. Representation at labour congresses came to favour the union bureaucracy, with only a minority of seats reserved for delegates elected at the grass roots. While the role of the unions in defence of the interests of the workers was emphasized anew in the heyday of the 1970 union elections, the more conservative approach prevailed again by 1973. Unions could make specific criticism of 'concrete' matters that were going wrong, but they were supposed to stay away from more autonomous political behaviour.

By the end of the 1970s, the membership of the mass organizations stabilized. The CDRs and the FMC encompassed about four-fifths of the adult population and of the adult women, respectively. Whereas the proportion of the relevant populations that belonged to these organizations rose until the mid-1970s, they remained fairly constant thereafter, subsequent growth in membership resulting mostly from demographic change. It became clear that about one-fifth of adult Cubans wanted nothing to do with the mass organizations, and vice versa.

Membership in the mass organization in the 1980s had become a prerequisite for a successful life in Cuba. Responsible positions were open only to those who were integrated into the revolutionary process by their membership in one or more such organizations. It was likely, therefore, that some proportion of the members did not support the regime but belonged to the mass organizations simply to make their own life easier; a substantial proportion of the 1980 exiles, for example, had belonged to such organizations. Some of the organizations, especially the labour unions, allocated certain resources: only those judged to have been vanguard workers had the right to acquire such consumer durables as sewing machines, refrigerators or television sets, and only they had priority access to scarce housing. Other workers could not acquire such goods even if they had the money.

The mass organizations thus became controllers of access to the good life – or at least to a bearable life.

The mass organizations and other political and bureaucratic institutions were subordinated to the party, a relationship which is made explicit in the Constitution of 1976. In the autumn of 1965, the party's name was changed again to the Communist Party of Cuba (PCC). At the same time, Fidel Castro unveiled the first one-hundred-member Central Committee, along with two smaller organs: the Political Bureau, responsible for the making of basic political decisions, and the Secretariat, charged with their implementation. Nevertheless, the party's influence remained limited for the balance of the decade. Not until the early 1970s were serious efforts made to turn it into an effective ruling Communist Party.

The party's first Congress was held in December 1975, the preparatory work for which was a major step forward to institutionalize PCC rule. The Congress approved party statutes, a programmatic platform and a number of statements or 'theses' on various subjects of national policy. It approved the draft of the new national Constitution, which was approved by a popular referendum in 1976. The Congress also approved the first five-year plan and other economic policies. The Central Committee was renovated and expanded to 112 members with a dozen alternates; new authority and activity were vested in the Political Bureau and Secretariat. Indeed, Cuba could be said to have had a functioning, ruling Communist Party only from the early 1970s when the preparations for this Congress were begun. A second party Congress was held in December 1980 and a third in February 1986. Each monitored, passed judgement, and largely ratified the previous half-decade's policies, renewing membership of the key party bodies, and approving new economic policies (including the second and third five-year plans) for the half-decade ahead.

The party's size grew from about 15,000 in 1962, when Aníbal Escalante fell, to 50,000 at the time of the foundation of the Communist Party in 1965. There were just over 100,000 members in 1970; slightly more than 200,000 on the eve of the first Congress; 434,143 on the eve of the second Congress; and 523,639 on the eve of the third Congress. In 1980 about 9 per cent of the population aged twenty-five and older belonged to the party.

The principal change in the composition of the Central Committee was the decline in the military's share of the membership, down among full members from 58 per cent in 1965 to 17 per cent in 1986. The bureaucracy's share of the Central Committee remained remarkably constant at about one-sixth of the membership until 1980, rising to more than one-quarter in 1986. The military's loss has been the politicians' gain. The share of professional politicians (including leaders of mass organizations) in the Central Committee rose from 17 per cent in 1965 to 41 per cent in 1986. The Central Committee membership was thus increasingly reflecting the need for routine government skills.

The military understandably had much influence in the 1960s. Cuba had rearmed quickly and massively to fight the United States. Many military commanders were the heroes of the revolutionary war of the late 1950s and had fought successfully against the internal counter-revolution and at the Bay of Pigs. Led by Raúl Castro, the armed forces had become the only truly well-organized segment of Cuban society in the 1960s. The military organized the party within its ranks, retaining political authority under the command and leadership of the officers, four-fifths of whom were party members by the early 1970s. The armed forces possessed the routine and procedure necessary for party-building whereas these were often lacking in civilian sectors in the radical period of the late 1960s. As a result, the government often relied on the military to perform social, economic and political tasks. These 'civic soldiers', competent in a wide array of fields, were consequently predominant in the party's ranks at all levels in the 1960s.

As the civilian party grew in the 1970s many 'civic soldiers' were transferred fully to civilian tasks, the armed forces concentrating on their military expertise and shedding many (though not all) strictly non-military activities. As the radical period faded, non-military modes of organization expanded, but the decline in the military share of the Central Committee did not mean that individuals who had been officers were removed from it. On the contrary, the rate of turnover in Central Committee membership was slow, and those who left the armed forces to serve in civilian party or government posts in the 1970s and 1980s remained Central Committee members.

The share of top party organs accounted for by the old Communist Party (PSP) members remained at about one-fifth, albeit declining slightly over time (former PSP members were generally older than the rest of the leadership and more likely to have failing health). Particularly in the 1960s, the PSP share was affected by the factional splits among top leaders, of which the two most dramatic were the dismissal of Aníbal Escalante as party Organization Secretary in 1962 and the uncovering of a 'microfaction' (also linked to Escalante) in 1968. PSP influence declined markedly in the late 1960s.

In late 1967, the top leadership discovered what was called a 'microfaction' within the Cuban Communist Party. It was composed primarily of former PSP members who believed that government and party policies at home and abroad were wrong. Led by Aníbal Escalante, the microfaction developed ties to Soviet and East European government and party officials. Once uncovered, those who belonged to the Central Committee were dropped; many others were expelled from the party, and the leaders of the microfaction were sent to prison for their crimes of opinion and association, although they had taken no other steps that could be construed as counter-revolutionary. Since their diagnosis of mistaken Cuban policies would eventually prove correct, they were punished for having the right insights at the wrong time.

Microfactionists or not, most former PSP members supported close relations with the Soviet Union and correct relations with most governments. They opposed attacks on Latin American Communist parties and were wary of guerrilla movements; they believed in the need for material incentives during a period of transition to socialism and considered that labour unions had to play a more prominent role in politics. The microfactionists argued that mere reliance on the will and on subjective assessments was imprudent and that it was necessary to understand objective conditions in Cuba and abroad. Arguing that central planning, budgets, financial cost-accounting and other such tools were essential to build socialism, they were skeptical of mass-mobilization campaigns that sought to replace these conventional policies. The microfaction demanded the greater use and institutionalization of party organs and other political organizations, supporting the reintroduction of elections and a Constitution. Former PSP members were not the only ones who held these beliefs, but they constituted the most obvious 'faction'. The changes in policies in the 1970s followed these PSP preferences quite consistently not because the old politicians had defeated their rivals of an earlier day but because Fidel Castro and his close associates became persuaded of the wisdom of their arguments.

Former PSP members who, unlike Aníbal Escalante, remained loyal to Fidel Castro, emerged with special influence in the 1970s, Blas Roca and Carlos Rafael Rodríquez being two of the party's long-standing leaders. Roca took charge of the drafting of a new constitution and other basic legislation as well as overseeing their implementation. He made decisive contributions to institutionalization in the 1970s. Rodríguez was the intellectual architect of the change in internal and international economic policies; in the 1970s and 1980s his advice was influential from relations with the United States to policies towards the arts and letters.

Among others who contributed to government reorganization, institutionalization and improved performance in the 1970s were education minister José Ramón Fernández, armed forces minister Raúl Castro, foreign trade minister Marcelo Fernández, Central Planning Board president Humberto Pérez, and interior minister Sergio del Valle. Marcelo Fernández, dismissed in the midst of the 1979–80 crisis, had diversified economic relations and had succeeded in thoroughly undermining the U.S. economic embargo policies against Cuba. Humberto Pérez had the thankless task of informing the government of basic economic truths, reorganizing the economy from the debacle of the 1960s. He endeavoured to bring supply and demand into balance, adopt the mechanisms common to centrally planned economies, stimulate increases in efficiency and productivity, and promote cost reductions, while seeking to enhance managerial and worker participation in economic affairs. The poor performance of the economy should be attributed to the difficulty of these tasks rather than to Pérez's inadequacies. Nonetheless, he was dismissed in 1985, when overall economic co-ordination tasks were given to Osmany Cienfuegos.

Interior minister Sergio del Valle's work cannot be assessed easily. His responsibility remained throughout to repress the opposition and to retain full political control at all costs. However, del Valle deserves credit for softening the harshness of authoritarian controls that had existed in the 1960s. According to the government's official figures, the number of political prisoners fell from about 20,000 in the mid-1960s to 4,000 in the mid-1970s, and to as few as 1,000 when del Valle was removed from his post in the midst of the 1979–80 crisis. The incidence of torture declined and changed in character during del Valle's tenure. Physical torture virtually disappeared and prison conditions improved although psychological torture remained an occasional tool. The police began to observe procedural safeguards to protect the rights of the accused. In the revitalized court system in the late 1970s, cases would be dismissed for lack of evidence or for violations of established procedures. The persistence of many internal security measures was still, of course, subject to criticism at the end of del Valle's tenure, but he had professionalized his service, enhanced the rule of law, and reduced arbitrariness.

Important changes in the organization of the government were introduced in the first half of the 1970s. In November 1972 the Council of Ministers was reorganized to create an executive committee comprising the Prime Minister and all the deputy prime ministers, each of whom would supervise several ministries. The executive committee became the government's key decision-making organ. An experiment in local government was also introduced in 1974 in Matanzas, one of Cuba's six provinces. These procedures would be applied with some variations nationwide under the constitution approved in 1976.

The Constitution of 1976 mandated the establishment of a new National Assembly with legislative powers, these having been vested in the Council of Ministers between 1959 and 1976. The National Assembly would elect the Council of State to function when the assembly was not in session. The president of the Council of State would also become the head of state and serve as head of the government (president of the Council of Ministers). Fidel Castro became head of state replacing Osvaldo Dorticós. Unlike other socialist constitutions, Cuba's requires that the head of state and the head of the government be the same person, a typical Latin American pattern.

A new political and administrative division of the national territory was also implemented in 1976. Instead of the six provinces inherited from the nineteenth century (Pinar del Río, La Habana, Matanzas, Las Villas, Camagüey, Oriente) there would be fourteen: Pinar del Río, La Habana, city of La Habana, Matanzas, Cienfuegos, Villa Clara, Sancti Spíritus, Ciego de Avila, Camagüey, Las Tunas, Granma, Holguín, Santiago de Cuba, and Guantánamo. The Isle of Pines, soon to be renamed the Isle of Youth, became a special municipality. The regions into which the provinces had been subdivided were abolished. There would be 169 municipalities. The most dramatic changes were the splintering of Oriente and of Las Villas provinces into four and three new provinces, respectively.

The Constitution also established elected provincial and municipal governments. The 1976 nationwide elections were the first since 1959. The only direct elections, however, were for members of the municipal assemblies, who themselves elected the executive committee for each municipal assembly, the delegates to the provincial assemblies, and the deputies of the National Assembly. Assembly membership at all levels was a part-time position, members retaining their jobs while serving on the assemblies. The National Assembly normally met twice a year, each session lasting two or three days. Such conditions made it a weak counterpart to government and party organizations.

The electoral law, and some of the procedures in the Constitution itself, further limited the impact of these changes. Self-nomination for elections was impossible and candidates were only nominated in assemblies by a show of hands. Campaigning by the candidates was prohibited; they could not address issues. Only the Communist Party, or the government, could campaign and address the issues, making it impossible for critics to exchange views and information. They could not associate as a party because the Constitution accorded that right only to the PCC. The party and government published biographies of the candidates, who could not veto what may be included in those biographies. At times the only recourse to avoid public humiliation, if nominated against the party's wishes, was to withdraw from an election contest.

The electoral law strengthened the party's control over the higher offices. The lists of nominees for provincial delegates, for executives at the municipal and provincial levels, and for national deputies, was prepared by nominating commissions led by the party. Party members accounted for more than nine-tenths of the membership of the National Assembly. Moreover, provincial delegates and National Assembly deputies did not have to be elected directly by the people to the municipal assemblies in the first instance. The nominating commissions might put forth anyone judged worthy. Approximately 44.5 per cent of National Assembly deputies elected in 1976 to a five-year term had never faced the electorate directly.

The municipal, provincial and national assemblies played a modest role in politics. Their effective powers were far less than appears from a reading of the Constitution. Debate in the National Assembly on the bills that could be used to control the executive branch, such as the annual plan or budget, was perfunctory and votes were typically unanimous. At the provincial or municipal levels, the constraints of extremely limited budgets and the extraordinary authority reserved for central state organs had limited assembly effectiveness. Nonetheless, the National Assembly featured freer and somewhat influential debates on issues other than macroeconomic policy or foreign and military policy. On such matters as common crime, environmental protection and family legislation deputies had some influence over the content of bills. At the local level, the job of municipal assembly delegates was not unlike that of an ombudsman. These delegates gathered citizen complaints and sought to break through bureaucratic obstacles to improve the delivery of government services to their constituents. Indeed, the contacting of public officials to solve local needs – the hallmark of political machines – became one of the most effective means of political participation in Cuba.

The stimulation of citizen complaints to correct local government errors, and the satisfaction of some demands, marked a fundamental difference between politics in the first fifteen years of revolutionary rule and those thereafter. Such protests had been limited, and at times repressed, in the earlier years when the only permissible mode of political participation was mass mobilization. In a more institutionalized authoritarian setting, the regime now relied on subtler policies. At the local level citizens were allowed – at times encouraged – to voice criticisms of specific problems; for such purposes, Cuba now had considerable freedom of expression. The authoritarian constraints, however, limited freedom of association at all levels. Critics of the regime were not allowed to associate in protest or criticism of government policies. Moreover, even at the local level, more general or abstract criticism of the government was frowned upon.

Further constraints on freedom of political expression existed at both the provincial and the national level. Since the spring of 1960 all mass media had been in state hands. Except for occasional letters-to-the-editor that resembled the specific criticism of local problems just mentioned, the mass media provided relentless (and often dull) support for regime policies and activities. There was somewhat greater though still limited freedom of expression to publish artistic and scholarly materials. In 1961, Fidel Castro summarized the regime's cultural policies in an ambiguous phrase: 'Within the revolution, everything; against the revolution, nothing'.[10] Material opposed to the revolution was not published; that which was not explicitly critical of the regime but produced by its known opponents was also not published. Material produced by those whose behaviour was judged unconventional and unacceptable by the government (e.g., actual or rumoured homosexual behaviour) had an uncertain fate; homosexuals suffered greatest hostility in the late 1960s and again in 1980. There was, however, some freedom of expression for persons who supported the Revolution politically and who wrote on topics other than those bearing on contemporary politics.

Especially in the 1960s, Cuba's policies did not emphasize 'socialist realism' as the dominant form of artistic production. In contrast to the

---

[10] Fidel Castro, *Palabras a los intelectuales* (Havana, 1961).

Soviet Union, there was freedom to choose artistic and literary forms. By the 1970s the government was giving preference in exhibitions and publications to those who focused on 'the socialist reality', although this could still be done through some forms of abstract painting. One troubling feature of government policies towards artists and scholars was the possibility that policy might shift and that what appeared 'safe' to an author might not to the censor. Thus, self-censorship, rather than cruder measures, became the main limitation on artistic and scholarly freedom of expression.

One form of intellectual political activity with a modest history was the exposition of theoretical Marxism–Leninism. The main texts in courses on Marxism–Leninism were the speeches of Fidel Castro and other home-grown products. However, after the 1970s more serious efforts were made to disseminate the more abstract theoretical knowledge of Marxist-Leninist classics through the party schools and publications and through research and writing in the universities and the mass media. There was a more conscious effort to relate these theoretical writings to the specific concerns of contemporary Cuba. The main national daily newspaper, *Granma*, the official organ of the Communist Party, founded in autumn of 1965 from the merger of the newspapers of the 26 of July Movement (*Revolución*) and of the PSP (*Noticias de Hoy*), usually devoted a page to articles on theoretical and historical topics. Marxism–Leninism became a required subject in the universities for all professions.

As the 1980s began the regime had clearly consolidated its rule. It might be described as a consultative oligarchy under an undisputed leader. Fidel Castro retained the pivotal role that had marked Cuban politics since 1959, but his delegation of some responsibility to close associates gave the regime a more oligarchic, rather than simply personal, quality. There was an established elite interlinked at the top of party state and government organs. Eleven of the sixteen members of the Political Bureau elected at the Second Party Congress in December 1980 were also members of the Council of Ministers; fourteen of the Political Bureau members belonged to the Council of State (where they constituted a majority). Of the fourteen members of the executive committee of the Council of Ministers, eight were also Political Bureau members. By the 1986 third party Congress the need for greater delegation was recognized. Although every Political Bureau member retained one other major elite post, only six of the fourteen were simultaneously members of the Councils of State and of ministers as well. Still, between two and three dozen people now occupied all the significant top jobs in party, state and government organs.

There now existed more clearly differentiated second and subsequent echelons of leadership where organizational specialists – in contrast to the generalists at the very top – predominated. These appointments specialized in technical economic issues, military matters or party questions, but they interlocked less. Historical factional splits, inherited from the pre-revolutionary period, also became less important. There was a fair opportunity for intra-elite debate and for the exercise of some influence through the party's Central Committee, the National Assembly and the routine relationships of enterprise managers to central ministries.

The political system concentrated decision-making powers very heavily at the top. Despite some trends towards decentralization in the mid-1970s, Cuba had still a highly centralized political system, where most fundamental decisions were made by a relatively small number of people in Havana, most of whom had held high posts for over twenty years. Power relations became more institutionalized than they had been in the 1970s thanks to the changes in the party, the mass organizations and the institutions of economic policy-making and implementation, especially central planning.

At the bottom of the political pyramid about one-fifth of the adult population was excluded from effective participation in the mass organizations because they were considered – by both themselves and the authorities – opponents of the regime. Although the levels of political repression against such people declined markedly in the 1970s, they increased again in late 1979 and 1980. Sergio del Valle was replaced as Minister of the Interior by his predecessor Ramiro Valdés, who restored, though not in full, some of the harsh internal security policies of the earliest years of the revolutionary rule. The Minister of Justice, the Attorney General, and the president of the Supreme Court were also replaced in the same period. They were responsible for the more 'lenient' exercise of police and court power earlier in the 1970s; they were more 'liberal' within the context of an authoritarian regime. In 1979–80 the government re-emphasized the pre-eminence of its power against social and political dissidents. (Valdés was dismissed as interior minister in December 1985 and from the Political Bureau in February 1986).

At the intermediate levels, managers now had greater discretion in the work place to hire, fire and discipline workers. They gained new, but limited, authority to dispose of enterprise profits, and they began to

demand more powers. The mass organizations began to display some
interest-group features, above all the ANAP lobby on behalf of the private
peasantry but also, though less effectively, FMC, the women's federation.
In such an increasingly hierarchical political system, established practition-
ers of organizational politics such as the armed forces could claim a rising
and disproportionate share of national resources, justified not only by the
'internationalist' missions acquired in the second half of the 1970s but also
by new U.S. threats in the 1980s.

One effect of the revolution in the 1960s was to break the correlation
between social class background and political power. Many of the formerly
powerful were dead or imprisoned, or had emigrated. Many of the newly
powerful came from humble origins; the revolution dramatically accelerat-
ing the circulation of elites in the early 1960s. By the 1980s, however,
there was mounting evidence of correlations between positions of power
and social rank, institutionalized revolutionary rule greatly diminishing
the circulation of elites. Revolutionary leaders who were strikingly
young – late twenties and early thirties – when they seized power in
1959, had aged, but their identities had changed little. The average age of
the Central Committee had been increasing about one year per year. New
Central Committee members tended to come from the same generation
and the same types of background. There was little real renewal.

Oligarchy and hierarchy had been reinforced under institutionalization
but more effective means for consultation were also developed. Gone were
the days when the only means of consultation was raising hands at a public
rally in response to Fidel Castro's persuasive exhortations. From the local
to the national level, there was now a more systematic effort to consult
those who might be affected by new policies, especially at the middle and
top ranks of power. Consultation had become the main channel for interest
group lobbying, although it was little more than symbolic in dealings
with the mass of the population, and it clearly possessed the potential to
attenuate the remaining arbitrary features of the authoritarian regime.

'Demand for orderliness', President Castro told the second party Congress, 'should never be neglected in a revolution'.[11] He thus summarized
the response of his government to the tumultuous events of 1980: economic crisis, political opposition and repression, and massive emigration.
He also signalled the increased importance of political stratification and
order as concerns of the leadership. The question for the years ahead would

[11] *Granma Weekly Review*. 28 December 1980, 13.

be whether the new demands for orderliness in the revolution competed with, overcame, or excluded the demands for a revolution within the revolution: the great slogan of the late 1960s. Were the dreams of the late 1950s, which turned the revolution into a national epic for many Cubans, to be realized through rising political and social stratification? Would Cuba respond in the future more to order or to revolution?

INTERNATIONAL RELATIONS

Still threatened by the United States after the settlement of the missile crisis in 1962 – Washington boycotted all economic relations with Cuba and sought to enlist the assistance of other governments to strangle Cuba's economy and thereby bring down its government – and still uncertain over the extent of Soviet commitment, the Cuban government fashioned a global foreign policy to defend its interests. The survival of revolutionary rule in Cuba, the leadership's top priority, required a foreign policy that was both global and activist. Cuba built a large and capable foreign service skilled in diplomacy, international economics, intelligence and military affairs. From the outset, the leadership also sought to use foreign policy to obtain resources for Cuba's social and economic transformation. The relationship with the Soviet Union was the centerpiece of both these priorities. At the same time, Havana sought to maintain good relations with as many governments as possible throughout the world. This policy, consistent with the effort to break out of the isolation that the U.S. government was seeking to impose on Cuba, held open the possibility of economic relations with non-communist countries. Another priority was to expand Cuba's influence over international leftist movements, whether formally organized in Communist parties or not. Cuban leaders believed they had led a genuine revolution to power. The establishment of Marxism–Leninism in Cuba, unlike in most of eastern Europe at the end of the Second World War, was not the by-product of the country's occupation by the Soviet armed forces. This home-grown Caribbean revolution, moreover, had not been led by the old Communist Party. Cuban revolutionaries thought they had some fundamental insights into how Third World revolutions might emerge and evolve toward Marxism–Leninism: in short, they could teach the Soviets a thing or two about how to support revolutions in the closing third of the twentieth century.

The Cuban leaders were interested not just in influence but also in the actual promotion of revolutions. Their future would be more secure in a world of many friendly anti-imperialist revolutionary governments. Revolutions, moreover, were on the cutting edge of history, and the future belonged to those who analyzed it correctly and acted accordingly. It was not enough to allow history to unfold – that had been the error of the old Communists – for peoples must make their own history, even if they cannot do so exactly as they please. It was the duty of revolutionaries to make the revolution. However, this position was often difficult to reconcile with the need to retain diplomatic relations with the broadest possible number of governments.

In the mid-1960s the Cuban government developed an independent foreign policy that brought it often into conflict with the Soviet Union. Cuba supported revolutionary movements vigorously in many Latin American countries and in Africa. Cuba gave material assistance to revolutionaries in most Central American and Andean countries, to those fighting the Portuguese empire in Africa, and also to friendly revolutionary governments such as those of the Congo (Brazzaville), Algeria and North Vietnam. In January 1966 Cuba hosted a Tricontinental Conference, from which were founded the Organization for Solidarity with the Peoples of Africa, Asia and Latin America (OSPAAL) and the Organization for Latin American Solidarity (OLAS). Based in Havana and staffed by Cubans, both supported revolutionary movements. Cuban leaders sharply criticized those who did not take up the armed struggle to bring about revolutionary victory; most Moscow-affiliated Communist parties in Latin American countries were assailed for their excessive caution, if not their cowardice.

If armed struggle was the way forward, then the Moscow-affiliated Venezuelan Communist Party, Castro declared, committed treason when it sought to end Venezuela's guerrilla war in 1967 and to reintegrate itself into more normal politics. But the commitment to the armed struggle, though essential, was not enough. Some who refused to conform to Cuban policies (as the revolutionary Yon Sosa in Guatemala) were denounced as Trotskyites. Cuba wanted to promote revolution, but it wanted even more to maintain and expand its influence over the left. It was willing to split the left, internationally and in particular countries, to maintain its primacy, even at the cost of jeopardizing revolutionary victory. These policies brought Havana into conflict with other governments, especially in Latin America. When Cuba was caught actively assisting Venezuelan revolutionaries the Venezuelan government brought charges of aggression that led to Cuba's condemnation under the terms of the Inter-American Treaty of Reciprocal Assistance (the Rio Pact) in 1964. Collective hemispheric sanctions were imposed on Cuba, requiring all signatories to suspend political and economic relations with Cuba. The United States and all Latin American countries (except Mexico) complied.

These policies also brought conflict to Soviet–Cuban relations. In addition to the conflict over the role of Moscow-affiliated Communist parties, Cuban leaders – especially the Minister of Industries, the Argentine-born hero of the revolutionary war, Ernesto 'Che' Guevara – criticized the USSR for its superpower behavior, and niggardly help to the Cuban Revolution. Soviet and East European products were called 'old junk'. The Cuban government seemed to hold its Soviet ally in contempt as an unrevolutionary country at home and abroad. Cubans had taken up the fallen standard of revolution. When the Cuban leadership linked the USSR and its allies to the microfaction, a Cuban–Soviet confrontation erupted early in 1968. The Soviet Union retaliated by slowing down the rate of delivery of petroleum products to Cuba, forcing the revolutionary government to impose a drastic rationing of petroleum products. The Soviets also withdrew most of their technical advisers. After difficult negotiations, the crisis was overcome in the summer 1968 when Prime Minister Castro unexpectedly acknowledged on television that he was about to endorse the Soviet and Warsaw Pact intervention in Czechoslovakia. This was the historic turning point in Soviet–Cuban relations, the subsequent improvement reaching its peak in co-operation in the African wars of the late 1970s.

Foreign policy faced other sharp problems in the late 1960s. The death of Che Guevara and other members of the Cuban Communist Party's Central Committee in the heartland of Bolivia where they had gone to spark a revolution represented a significant set-back. More generally, the strategy of promoting revolution through armed struggle failed throughout Latin America, consolidating either democratic regimes, as in Venezuela, or dynastic tyrannies, as in Nicaragua. Non-violent strategies that promised change appeared more viable: a left-leaning military government came to power in Peru late in 1968 and a broad coalition of the Chilean left won the presidential elections in 1970.

Cuban relations with the People's Republic of China also soured during the mid-1960s. Notwithstanding the many similarities in outlook and policy between the leaderships and despite the considerable Chinese economic aid to Cuba in the early 1960s, relations deteriorated when the Chinese leadership demanded full Cuban support in the Sino-Soviet dispute and lobbied Cuban military and party personnel directly. When the economies of both countries deteriorated in the mid-1960s there was intensified commercial conflict, and although trade and other relations were never cut off altogether, they were sharply reduced. Bilateral political relations continued to be poor after early 1966.

Despite these difficulties, the most fundamental priorities of Cuban foreign policy were met. Revolutionary rule survived, in itself a remarkable achievement. The pattern of policy gave priority to good relations with the Soviet Union over support for revolution. The Cuban government could not have survived in power without Soviet support, which had increased since the late 1960s. A major agreement signed in December 1972 postponed until January 1986 payments of interest and principal on all Soviet credits granted to Cuba before January 1973, repayments then being extended into the twenty-first century. (In fact, in 1986 repayments were deferred for several more years). Soviet credits to cover bilateral trade deficits for 1973–5 were granted free of interest, with the principal to be repaid from 1986. Between 1960 and 1974 Soviet subsidies of bilateral trade deficits with Cuba totalled approximately $3.8 billion. These deficits would have been larger if the Soviet Union had not also subsidized Cuban sugar exports to the USSR during most years, to the tune of about a billion dollars during the 1960s. In 1976, in partial reward for Cuba's military daring and success in Angola, the Soviet Union again agreed to subsidize Cuban sugar sales through a complex formula that stipulated a price five or six times greater than that prevailing on the world market. In addition, the Soviet Union subsidized the price of the petroleum it sold to Cuba and of the nickel it bought from Cuba. After 1976, Soviet subsidies remained at a very high level, accounting for no less than a tenth of Cuba's gross product per year.

These subsidies predictably tightened Cuban–Soviet trade relations. Whereas commerce with the USSR accounted for an average of 45 per cent of Cuban trade up to 1975, it exceeded 60 per cent in the early 1980s. Cuban trade also increased with Eastern European countries when they agreed to subsidize sugar prices. These shifts were also caused by Cuba's difficulties in trading with hard-currency markets (most Cuban trade with the Soviet Union and East Europe was, in effect, barter trade with imputed prices). In addition, Cuba has received Soviet assistance for economic development projects, the training of Cuban technical personnel in the USSR, and the stationing of Soviet technical advisers in Cuba.

A notable element of Soviet assistance to Cuba was military. In addition to the military shield provided by the Soviet Union against the United

States, Moscow developed the Cuban armed forces into Latin America's premier military establishment. No other armed force in the region could match the skill, experience and sophistication of the Cuban army and air force. The Cuban navy was the only service whose development still lagged. Soviet arms transfers were free of charge, the equipment and modernization of the Cuban armed forces reaching its peak in a large build-up during the early 1980s.

A new phase of Soviet–Cuban military co-operation opened with Cuba's decision to send eventually 36,000 troops to support the Popular Movement for the Liberation of Angola (MPLA) in the civil war that broke out in that country in 1975–6. Although Cuba's entry into that victorious war would not have been possible without Soviet support, the chronology of engagement, the pattern of deployment and the testimony of key witnesses suggest that Cuba and the MPLA – rather than the USSR – took the major decisions. In January 1978, responding to a request from the Ethiopian government faced with a Somali invasion that had occupied a substantial portion of Ethiopian territory, thousands of Cuban troops, supported and led by Soviet and East German officers in addition to Cuban officers, helped repel the Somali invasion. The pattern in this case suggests that the Soviet Union and Ethiopia took the lead in formulating and implementing these policies.

In short, the Soviet–Cuban alliance by the 1980s was close and complex, responding to the perceived interests of both allies, respecting the independence of each and allowing each to formulate its own policies in close collaboration with the other. Although Cuban victories in African wars would not have been achieved without Soviet support, it is also true that Soviet victories would not have been achieved without Cuban forces.

Appreciable success was registered in improving state-to-state relations in general. Even in the years of a radical foreign policy in the 1960s, Cuba had maintained good trade relations with several Western European states. The case of Franco's Spain was noteworthy. From 1963 until Franco's death in 1975, Cuba had excellent economic relations with that country, desisting from the promotion of revolution there in order to maintain a mutually valuable official relationship. Cuba also retained correct diplomatic relations with the Mexican government, eschewing the temptation to support anti-government leftist protests in 1968–71. In the early 1970s Cuba moved steadfastly to improve its relations with most governments. Economic relations with Western European countries and Japan improved further as the Cuban economy recovered from the ravages of the 1960s. In 1975 the collective inter-American political and economic sanctions were lifted, and several Latin American countries developed trade relations with Cuba. Mexican and Argentine trade with Cuba became important over the next five years, and even relations with the United States began to improve. Washington voted to lift collective sanctions and modified its own legislation to eliminate third-party sanctions embedded in U.S. economic embargo policies against Cuba. The Ford administration and the Cuban government held bilateral discussions in 1975, and although these talks were interrupted by the Angolan war, they were resumed in 1977 at the beginning of the Carter presidency. The new talks led to a series of modest bilateral agreements and to the establishment of diplomatic 'interest sections' by each country in the other's capital city. Although most of these procedures endured, relations began to deteriorate again in the wake of Cuba's entry into the Ethiopian–Somali war in 1978.

Cuban relations with Africa and Asia also improved in the 1970s. Cuba had joined the so-called Non-aligned Movement in 1961, and despite its increasingly close military alliance with the Soviet Union, Cuba became the movement's leader for a three-year term at the 1979 summit meeting of heads of state in Havana. Relations with these countries were significantly influenced by the deployment of thousands of Cubans serving in foreign-assistance missions. In the early 1980s some 15,000 Cubans served in overseas civilian missions in some three dozen countries; tasks in construction, health and education predominated.[12] In addition, about 35,000 troops and military advisers (including security experts) were ordinarily posted overseas in about two dozen countries (most were in Angola and Ethiopia). Relative to Cuba's population, the overseas armies represented a larger deployment than that of the United States at the peak of the Vietnam war. Cuba's sizeable military deployment in Angola endured for the same length as the U.S. wartime commitment in Vietnam.

[12] Cuban foreign assistance missions have operated in the following countries, among others, at the request of their governments: Chile, Peru, Panama, Nicaragua, Jamaica, Guyana, Grenada, Suriname, Algeria, Libya, Ethiopia, Somalia, Uganda, Tanzania, Seychelles, Zambia, Ghana, São Tomé and Príncipe, Mozambique, Angola, Zimbabwe, Congo, Nigeria, Benin, Burkina, Faso, Malagasy, Burundi, Equatorial Guinea, Guinea, Guinea-Bissau, Cape Verde, Sierre Leone, Mali, South Yemen, Syria, Iraq, Vietnam, Laos, and Kampuchea. In some of these, such as Libya and Iraq, Cubans are paid for their services, often working on construction or public-health projects, so that the relationship resembles that of a transnational firm selling services rather than foreign assistance.

The most decisive new initiative in foreign policy was the support from 1977 for the Sandinista insurgency against Anastasio Somoza's rule in Nicaragua, the first substantial commitment to promote insurgency in the Americas in a decade. After revolutionary victory in Nicaragua in July 1979, Cuba developed extremely close relations with the Sandinista government and also with the revolutionary government that came to power in Grenada in March 1979. Havana sent several thousand civilian and military personnel to Nicaragua and several hundred to Grenada. By its own admission, Cuba also provided political, military and economic support to the insurgents in El Salvador, especially in 1980 and early 1981.

Revolutionary success in Nicaragua was the first in Latin America since the Cuban revolution itself. It frightened neighbouring governments and, above all, that of the United States, which, following the inauguration of Ronald Reagan in January 1981, once again threatened Cuba with military invasion. Cuban reservists fought courageously (though to no avail) against the U.S. troops that invaded Grenada in October 1983 — the first such military clash in a quarter of a century.

If many internationally active Cubans fought bravely for their country in African fields and served foreign-assistance missions in three continents, nearly a million Cubans showed courage in breaking with their government, surmounting its controls and emigrating. The first wave of emigration occurred, as we have seen, in the immediate aftermath of the Revolution and came to an abrupt end in 1962; the second, from late 1965 until it tapered off early in the 1970s. The third wave of emigration occurred in one dramatic outburst in the spring of 1980. After several thousand Cubans had broken into the Peruvian embassy in Havana, the government allowed Cuban-Americans from the United States to come in small boats across the Florida Straits to Mariel harbor to pick up friends and relatives, provided they were also willing to ferry to the United States a substantial minority of people whom the Cuban government called 'scum'. These were rounded up by internal security forces or released from Cuban jails for what amounted to deportation from their own country. After Havana, Miami now became the city with the largest Cuban population.

The Cuban Revolution had burst on the world from a small Caribbean island, gradually becoming one of the central issues in international affairs. Cuba's foreign policy succeeded in ensuring the survival of revolutionary rule and obtaining resources from the Soviet Union. It had influence over many African governments but was less successful in turning insurgencies into revolutionary governments in the Americas. Its leaders commanded world attention; its policies had to be monitored by statesmen everywhere; its people could be found throughout the globe. The stage of the Cuban Revolution had become universal as its concerns and policies impinged on millions of its friends and foes in many countries.

CUBA IN THE LATE 1980S AND EARLY 1990S

Cuba's fortunes began to change in the late 1980s. The economic recession that had begun in 1986 lingered for the remainder of the 1980s. One reason for the recession was the decline in labour productivity as Cuban workers responded adversely to the policies of 'rectification' announced in 1986 that sought to de-emphasize the role of certain material incentives for work. Beginning in 1989, Cuba also began to feel the full force of the decomposition of the communist regimes in the Soviet Union and in Eastern Europe. From 1989 to 1991, for example, Cuban imports of petroleum products from the U.S.S.R. dropped by two-thirds, forcing a severe rationing throughout Cuba's economy of many products dependent on energy inputs. All the Eastern European countries cancelled their economic assistance programmes and reduced their trade with Cuba; East Germany's incorporation into a larger Germany led to a particularly drastic reduction of Cuban trade. From 1989 to 1991 the U.S.S.R. reduced both its economic subsidies and the transfer of weapons free of charge to Cuba; both of these kinds of subsidies were eventually cancelled by the Russian Federation and by other successor states to the former Soviet Union. Cuban trade continued with most of the successor states, although generally at international market prices and at levels well below those of 1989.

Partly in response first to the end of the Cold War and then to the collapse of the Soviet Union, but also thanks to important Cuban battlefield successes, Cuban troops returned home. Withdrawal from Ethiopia was completed by the beginning of 1990, prior to full withdrawal of Soviet troops as well as prior to the collapse of Col. Mengistu Haile Mariam's government. Cuban troops had successfully prevented Somalia's conquest of the Ogaden. By the spring of 1990 Cuban troops and military advisers had withdrawn from Nicaragua at the request of the government that replaced the Sandinistas after their defeat in the 1990 national elections. Cuban troops had successfully advised the Sandinista military in their battlefield defeat of the 'contra' military bands. Withdrawal from Angola was completed in May 1991. Cuban troops had stopped the South African military invasion of Angola and bloodied the South African armed forces, thereby contributing powerfully to a process of negotiation that culminated in South Africa's full withdrawal from Angola and its granting of independence to Namibia, as well as to the beginning of the end of the apartheid regime in South Africa itself. Angola's political regime, however, had begun to change contrary to Cuba's own preferences; the Angolan government moved to open its economy to market forces and to open its politics to multiparty competition.

Whether as a result of battlefield victories that no longer required a Cuban military presence or at the request of governments and as a result of international negotiations, the return of Cuban troops to their homeland in the early 1990s put an end to a remarkable chapter in Cuba's international relations and markedly reduced Cuba's influence in the world beyond its boundaries. This decline in Cuban influence overseas was accelerated also in the early 1990s by the formal end of Augusto Pinochet's dictatorship in Chile and by the negotiated end of internal warfare in El Salvador. By Fidel Castro's own admission, to the very end Cuba had supported armed violence against the governments of both countries. If for thirty years Cuba had been able to behave as an unlikely 'superpower', by the early 1990s it had once again become just an island in the sun.

The changes in domestic politics in the late 1980s and early 1990s were no less momentous. President Fidel Castro re-asserted his personal power and vision to prevent Cuban politics from evolving in the direction taken in Eastern Europe and in the Soviet Union, dismissing officials who, for various reasons not related only to those external changes, did not agree with his preferences. Whereas Cuba's top leadership had been remarkably stable from the mid-1960s to the mid-1980s, the membership of the Communist Party's Political Bureau was thoroughly revamped from the mid-1980s to the early 1990s. Nearly all the giants of domestic Cuban politics from the 1970s and early 1980s were demoted or disgraced. At the end of the Fourth Party Congress in October 1991 only five of the Political Bureau's members from 1975 were still at their posts.

In the summer of 1989 Fidel Castro recognized that corruption had spread throughout the upper echelons of the regime. Division General Arnaldo Ochoa, decorated Hero of the Republic of Cuba and architect of Cuban military victories in wars in Ethiopia and Angola, was arrested and shot for having committed acts of corruption; so too were three high-ranking officers in Ministry of the Interior, which was put in receivership and thoroughly purged by Army Corps General Abelardo Colomé. Many other instances of corruption, albeit less dramatic, surfaced in other parts of the government, signalling to Cubans that power had corrupted many leaders who thirty years earlier had come to office promising to end corruption.

By the early 1990s the heightened economic austerity caused a sharp decline in living standards, though the government sought to protect its historic accomplishments in health and in education. Most goods and services came once again to be severely rationed. At the same time, political repression against dissident groups became tougher; the number of 'prisoners of conscience' rose. Political opposition groups remained small and divided, however. Public opinion polls conducted by the Communist Party itself, or by scholars working in Cuban think-tanks, showed a rise in disagreement over fundamental policies between government leaders and ordinary citizens; a loss of prestige by the Communist Party as an institution amidst the population; and sharp criticism of many government services as well as of the inadequate supply of goods. The same polls, however, showed considerable public admiration for many of the government's social policies as well as continuing high respect for many well-regarded individuals who remained Communist Party members.

At the beginning of 1992 Cuba's future remained uncertain. Only one thing seemed clear: living standards, at least in the short term, would fall for most ordinary citizens no matter who governed their country under whatever kind of regime.

BIBLIOGRAPHICAL ESSAYS

1. CUBA, C. 1750–C. 1860

Hugh Thomas, *Cuba: The Pursuit of Freedom* (London, 1971), is a general history of Cuba since 1762. Raymond Carr, *Spain, 1808–1939* (Oxford, 1966), is the best general history of Spain for this period. On the Bourbon reforms in Cuba, see Allan J. Kuethe, *Cuba, 1753–1815: Crown, Military and Society* (Knoxville, Tenn., 1986). A history of U.S.–Cuban relations to 1895, coloured by twentieth-century guilt, is Philip Foner, *A History of Cuba and Its Relations with the U.S.*, 2 vols. (New York, 1962–3). Ramiro Guerra y Sánchez, *Sugar and Society in the Caribbean: An Economic History of Cuban Agriculture*, trans. Marjorie Urquidi (New Haven, Conn., 1964), and Fernando Ortiz, *Cuban Counterpoint: Tobacco and Sugar*, trans. Harriet de Onis (New York, 1947), are brilliant and suggestive essays by great Cuban writers. Planter society is well analysed in Roland T. Ely, *Cuando reinaba su majestad el azúcar: Estudio histórico-sociológico de una tragédia latinoamericana* (Buenoas Aires, 1963), a major work of historical reconstruction largely based on the papers of the Drake and Terry families. See also Franklin W. Knight, 'Origins of Wealth and the Sugar Revolution in Cuba, 1750–1850', *Hispanic American Historical Review* 57, no. 2 (1977), pp. 236–53. Laird W. Bergad, *Cuban Rural Society in the Nineteenth Century: The Social and Economic History of Monoculture in Matanzas* (Princeton, 1990), is an important provincial study. The sugar industry is best studied from a technical point of view in Manuel Moreno Fraginals, *El ingenio*, vol. 1 (Havana, 1964), Eng. trans. *The Sugarmill: The Socioeconomic Complex of Sugar in Cuba 1760–1860* (New York, 1976). The slave trade to Cuba in the nineteenth century, and its abolition, has been adequately covered in David Murray, *Odious Commerce: Britain, Spain and the Abolition of the Cuban Slave Trade* (Cambridge, 1980), while the Spanish side of the abolition of both the slave trade and slavery has been analysed in Arthur F. Corwin, *Spain and the abolition of slavery in Cuba, 1817–1886* (Austin, 1967). See also Raúl Cepero Bonilla, *Azúcar y abolición* (Havana, 1948). Important studies of slavery in Cuba include H. H. S. Aimes, *A History of Slavery in Cuba, 1511–1868* (New York, 1907), a workmanlike, if occasionally misleading, pioneering work of scholarship; Herbert S. Klein, *Slavery in the Americas: A Comparative Study of Virginia and Cuba* (Chicago, 1967), which suffers from a disposition to believe Spanish slave laws meant what they said; Franklin W. Knight, *Slave Society in Cuba During the Nineteenth Century* (Madison, Wisc., 1970); Gwendolyn Hall, *Social Control in Slave Plantation Societies: A Comparison of Saint Domingue and Cuba* (Baltimore, 1971); Verena Martinez-Alier, *Marriage, Class and Colour in Nineteenth-Century Cuba: A Study of Racial Attitudes and Sexual Values in a Slave Society* (Cambridge, 1974); and J. Pérez de la Riva, *El barracón: Esclavitud y capitalismo en Cuba* (Barcelona, 1978). Kenneth T. Kiple, *Blacks in Colonial Cuba, 1774–1899* (Gainesville, 1976), is a rich compilation of census data on blacks, slave and free. On U.S. attitudes to Cuba in the middle of the nineteenth century, besides Foner, see Basil Rauch, *American Interests in Cuba, 1848–1855* (New York, 1948), and Robert E. May, *The Southern Dream of a Caribbean Empire, 1854–1861* (Baton Rouge, 1973).

2. CUBA, C. 1860 – C. 1930

Among general histories, the *Enciclopedia de Cuba* (12 vols., Madrid, 1975), edited in exile by several Cuban scholars and writers, is an uneven work which contains some valuable essays. Ramiro Guerra y Sánchez et al. *Historia de la nación cubana*, 10 vols. (Havana, 1952), is a compilation of essays by different authors which occasionally provides excellent information. Jorge Ibarra, *Historia de Cuba* (Havana, 1968), is a Marxist interpretation. Leví Marrero, *Cuba: Economía y sociedad,* 9 vols. (Madrid, 1976), contains the results of some excellent research but is in desperate need of organization. José Duarte Oropesa, *Historiología cubana,* 5 vols. (n.p., 1969–70), is a good contribution, rendered less valuable by the author's reluctance to display his sources. Hortensia Pichardo, *Documentos para la historia de Cuba,* 4 vols. (Havana, 1976), selected with some Marxist bias, includes some otherwise inaccessible documents. José Manuel Pérez Cabrera, *Historiografía de Cuba* (Mexico, 1952), is a valuable guide to the literature on Cuba in the nineteenth century. Fernando Portuondo, *Histo-*

ria de Cuba (Havana, 1957), was considered the best textbook in Cuba until 1960. Oscar Pino Santos, *Historia de Cuba: Aspectos fundamentales* (Havana, 1964), seeks to explain Cuba's economic development or lack of it from a Marxist perspective. Emeterio S. Santovenia and Raúl M. Shelton, *Cuba y su historia*, 4 vols. (Miami, 1965), is a clear and reliable work by a Cuban and an American historian. Jaime Suchliki, *Cuba: From Columbus to Castro* (New York, 1974), is a good, unpretentious overview of Cuban history. In spite of a certain tendency to disregard Cuban sources, Hugh Thomas, *Cuba: The Pursuit of Freedom* (London, 1971), remains the most complete history of the island from 1762 to 1968. The most recent general history is Louis A. Pérez, Jr., *Cuba: Between Reform and Revolution* (New York, 1988).

On relations with the United States, Russell H. Fitzgibbon, *Cuba and the United States, 1900–1935* (Menasha, Wisc., 1935; rpt. New York, 1964), is a well-documented and serious attempt to analyse the different factors which shaped Cuban–American relations while the Platt Amendment was still in force. Herminio Portell Vilá, *Historia de Cuba en sus relaciones con los Estados Unidos y España*, 4 vols. (Havana, 1939), is an important study which goes beyond the scope of its title. Philip S. Foner, *A History of Cuba and Its Relations with the United States*, 2 vols. (New York, 1962–3), is an ambitious, well-researched though anti-American work. Lester D. Langley, *The Cuban Policy of the United States: A Brief History* (New York, 1968), and Louis A. Pérez, Jr., *Cuba and the United States: Ties of Singular Intimacy* (Athens, Ga., 1990), are excellent surveys. In Robert F. Smith, *The United States and Cuba: Business and Diplomacy, 1917–1960* (New Haven, Conn. 1960), published under the impact of the Cuban revolution, the author demonstrates how American economic interests have affected and distorted U.S.–Cuban policy. See also Jules R. Benjamin, *The United States and Cuba: Hegemony and Dependent Development, 1880–1934* (Pittsburgh, Pa. 1977). Still valuable is Dana G. Munro, *Intervention and Dollar Diplomacy in the Caribbean, 1900–1921* (Princeton, N.J., 1964).

Ramiro Guerra y Sánchez, *Sugar and Society in the Caribbean: An Economic History of Cuban Agriculture* (New Haven, Conn., 1964), originally published in Cuba in 1927, is an indictment of sugar's impact on the island's social and economic conditions; it has had a profound influence on Cuban studies. Leland H. Jenks, *Our Cuban Colony* (New York, 1928), is a classic on the impact of American economic imperialism in Cuba. Raymond L. Buell et al., *Problems of the New Cuba* (New York, 1935), is perhaps the best study on the origins of Cuba's economic problems in the twentieth century. Roland T. Ely, *Cuando reinaba su majestad el azúcar: Estudio histórico-sociológico de una tragédia latinomericana* (Buenos Aires, 1963), is an indispensable work on Cuba's sugar development. H. E. Friedlander, *Historia económica de Cuba* (Havana, 1944), is an interesting but incomplete study of Cuba's economic history, limited essentially to the nineteenth century. Julián Alienes y Urosa, *Características fundamentales de la economía cubana* (Havana, 1950), is an important contribution to understanding Cuba's economic problems from colonial times to 1940. Lowry Nelson, *Rural Cuba* (Minneapolis, 1950), is a pioneer study on the agrarian situation in Cuba in the first half of the twentieth century. José Alvarez et al., *A Study on Cuba* (Coral Gables, Fla., 1965), is a serious piece of research, full of reliable data and debatable interpretations. Raúl Cepero Bonilla, *Azúcar y abolición* (Havana, 1948), is a study of the economic roots of abolitionist and autonomist movements in the nineteenth century. Rebecca J. Scott, *Slave Emancipation in Cuba: The Transition to Free Labor, 1860–1899* (Princeton, 1985), is the outstanding work on the abolition of slavery in Cuba and its aftermath. Julio Le Riverend, *Historia económica de Cuba* (Havana, 1971), is a cautious Marxist interpretation of Cuba's economic evolution until 1940. Oscar Pino Santos, *El asalto a Cuba por la oligarquía financiera yanki* (Havana, 1973), is interesting, in spite of the vehement title, because it explores the presence and negative influence in Cuba of non-American capitalist groups. For a full discussion of the Cuban sugar industry in the period *c.* 1860–*c.* 1930, see Manuel Moreno Fraginals, 'Plantation economies and societies in the Spanish Caribbean, 1860–1930', in Leslie Bethell (ed.), *Cambridge History of Latin America*, vol. IV (Cambridge, 1986).

The two classic histories of the Ten Years' War (1868–78) by Cuban historians are Ramiro Guerra y Sánchez, *Guerra de los Diez Años* (Havana, 1950), and Francisco Ponte Domínguez, *Historia de la Guerra de los Diez Años* (Havana, 1972). Among a number of biographies José L. Franco, *Antonio Maceo: Apuntes para una historia de su vida*, 3 vols., (Havana, 1973), and Benigno Souza, *Máximo Gómez, el generalísimo* (Havana, 1953), deserve mention. The political ideas and legislative problems of the Cuban rebels are studied in Enrique Hernández Corujo, *Revoluciones cubanas: Organización civil y política* (Havana, 1929), and *Historia constitucional de Cuba* (Havana, 1960); Ramón Infiesta, *Historia constitucional de Cuba* (Havana, 1942); and Andrés Lazcano y Mazón, *Las constituciones de Cuba* (Madrid, 1952). For the texts of the different constitutions, see Leonel Antonio de la Cuesta and Rolando Alum Linera (eds.), *Constituciones cubanas, 1812–1962* (New York, 1974).

The most recent account of the period between the Ten Years' War and the War of Independence (1895–8) and United States occupation is Louis A. Pérez, *Cuba betwen Empires, 1878–1902* (Pittsburgh, Pa., 1983). See also two articles by Pérez, 'Toward Dependency and Revolution: The Political Economy of Cuba between Wars, 1878–1895', *Latin American Research Review* 18 (1983), pp. 127–42, and 'Vagrants, Beggars and Bandits: The Social Origins of Cuban Separatism, 1878–1895', *American Historical Review* 90 (1985) pp. 1092–121. The *autonomistas* have been studied, with excessive emphasis on the philosophical influences upon them, in Antonio Martínez Bello, *Orígen y meta del autonomismo: Exégesis de Montoro* (Havana, 1952); see also Antonio Sánchez de Bustamante y Montoro, *La ideología autonomista* (Havana, 1934) and, an exposition of the party's aims, Rafael Montoro, *Ideario autonomista* (Havana, 1938). On banditry, see Louis A. Pérez, Jr., *Lords of the Mountain: Social Banditry and Peasant Protest in Cuba, 1878–1918* (Pittsburgh, Pa., 1989), and Rosalie Schwartz, *Lawless Liberators: Political Banditry and Cuban Independence* (Durham, N.C., 1989).

Rafael Pérez Delgado, *1898, el año del desastre* (Madrid, 1976), reaches some sombre conclusions on the condition of the Spanish forces and the behaviour of the Spanish government and press. Mercedez Cervera Rodríguez, *La guerra naval del 98 en su planeamiento y en sus consecuencias* (Madrid, 1977), and José Cervera Pery, *Marina y política en la España del siglo XIX* (Madrid, 1979), are useful modern studies. José Manuel Allende Salazar, *El 98 de los americanos* (Madrid, 1974), is a serious attempt by a Spanish historian to understand the American side. A general background to Spanish politics is provided by Melchor Fernández Almagro, *Historia política de la España contemporánea*, 2 vols. (Madrid, 1959), and Pedro Gómez Aparicio, *Historia del periodismo español*, 2 vols. (Madrid, 1971).

There are four biographies of José Martí in English: Jorge Mañach, *Martí: Apostle of Freedom* (New York, 1950); Felix Lizaso, *Martí, Martyr of Cuban Independence* (Albuquerque, N.Mex., 1953); Richard Butler Gray, *José Martí, Cuban Patriot* (Gainesville, Fla., 1962); and John M. Kirk, *Martí: Mentor of the Cuban Nation* (Tampa, Fla., 1983). See also Christopher Abel and Nissa Torrents (eds.), *José Martí, Revolutionary Democrat* (Durham, N.C., 1986). Encumbered by philosophical quotations but useful is Roberto Agramonte, *Martí y su concepción del mundo* (San Juan, Puerto Rico, 1971). Emilio Roig de Leuchsenring, *Martí anti-imperialista*

(Havana, 1961), and Philip S. Foner (ed.), *José Martí, Inside the Monster: Writings on the United States and American Imperialism* (New York, 1975), stress Martí's well-known anti-imperialism. From a different perspective, but less scholarly, Rafael Esténger, *Martí frente al comunismo* (Miami, 1966), studies Martí's rejection of Marxism. *Martí: El héroe y su acción revolucionaria* (Mexico, 1966), by the Argentine writer Ezequiel Martínez Estrada, is a more balanced vision of Martí's radicalism. For a short bilingual collection of Martí's ideas, see Carlos Ripoll, *José Martí* (New York, 1980). Martí's writings can be consulted in his *Obras completas*, 2 vols. (Havana, 1956), or in the twenty-two-volume edition published in Havana in 1973.

Among the older American studies of the Spanish–American war, Walter Millis, *The Martial Spirit: A study of the War with Spain* (New York, 1931), remains important. Frank Freidel, *The Splendid Little War* (Boston, 1958), is more important for the illustrations than the analysis. Philip S. Foner, *The Spanish–Cuban–American War and the Birth of American Imperialism*, 2 vols. (New York, 1972), while showing the Marxist orientation of the author, has the merit of offering the Cuban side in the conflict. Julius Pratt, *Expansionists of 1898* (Baltimore, 1936), is a classic study on the ideas and economic interests behind the war. See also, more recently, Ernest R. May, *Imperial Democracy: The Emergence of America as a Great Power* (New York, 1973), and Charles S. Campbell, *The Transformation of American Foreign Relations, 1865–1900* (New York, 1976).

David F. Healy, *The United States in Cuba, 1898–1902* (Madison, 1963), is the best American study on the subject. Emilio Roig de Leuchsenring, *Historia de la Enmienda Platt*, 2 vols. (Havana, 1935; 2nd ed. 1961) is extremely anti-American. A more objective evaluation is provided in Manuel Márquez Sterling, *Proceso histórico de la Enmienda Platt (1897–1934)* (Havana, 1941). On the emergence of an ephemeral Socialist party under American occupation, see José Rivero Muñiz, *El primer Partido Socialista cubano* (Las Vilas, Cuba, 1962); Eduardo J. Tejera, *Diego Vicente Tejera, patriota, poeta y pensador cubano* (Madrid, 1981), is a biography of the founder of the Socialist party. On the impact of war and occupation on agrarian structures, see Louis A. Pérez, Jr., 'Insurrection, Intervention and the Transformation of Land Tenure Systems in Cuba, 1895–1902', *Hispanic American Historical Review* 65 (1985) pp. 229–54.

General works on the Republic, 1902–33, include Carleton Beals, *The Crime of Cuba* (Philadelphia, 1933), written when dictator Machado was in power; the author blames American economic penetration for the Cuban political tragedy. Charles E. Chapman, *History of the Cuban Republic* (New York, 1927), is a historical reflection of the island conditions as seen by an American at a time when nationalism was at a low ebb and pessimism was rampant in Cuba. Louis A. Pérez, Jr., *Cuba under the Platt Amendment, 1902–1934* (Pittsburgh, Pa., 1986), is the outstanding work of modern scholarship by a North American historian. An interesting Cuban study is Jorge Ibarra, *Un análisis psicosocial del cubano, 1898–1925* (Havana, 1985). Louis A. Pérez, *Army and Politics in Cuba, 1898–1958* (Pittsburgh, Pa., 1975), is an interesting account of the rise and fall of the Cuban army, but stronger on the period after 1933. Mario Riera Hernández, *Cuba republicana, 1898–1958* (Miami, 1974), provides a useful chronology and political guide. On Estrada Palma, the first president of the Republic, see Carlos Márquez Sterling, *Don Tomás: Biografía de una época* (Havana, 1953). A valuable defence of the Magoon administration, so severely criticized by the majority of Cuban historians, is provided by David A. Lockmiller, *Magoon in Cuba* (Chapel Hill, N.C., 1938). The best study on the period is Allan Reed Millet, *The Politics of Intervention: The Military Occupation of Cuba, 1906–1909* (Columbus, Ohio, 1968).

The period from 1908 to 1925, covering the presidencies of José Miguel Gómez, Mario G. Menocal and Alfredo Zayas, has been neglected by Cuban historians. Louis A. Pérez, *Intervention, Revolution, and Politics in Cuba, 1913–1921* (Pittsburgh, Pa., 1978) is an excellent study of the period, demonstrating how Cuban politicians learned to 'manipulate' American diplomacy, but making some sweeping generalizations about Cuban politics. Leon Primelles, *Crónica cubana, 1915–1918* (Havana, 1955), is a detailed chronology of Menocal's last years in power. José Rivero Muñiz examines the beginning of organized labour under the Republic in *El movimiento laboral cubano durante el período 1906–1911* (Las Villas, Cuba, 1962). On the rebellion of black groups in 1912, see Serafín Portuondo Linares, *Los independientes de color*, 2nd ed. (Havana, 1951), and Rafael Fermoselle, *Política y color: La guerrita de 1912* (Montevideo, 1974).

Machado's government and the revolutionary episode of 1933 have attracted considerable scholarly attention. See, for example, Luis E. Aguilar, *Cuba 1933: Prologue to Revolution* (Ithaca, N.Y., 1972); Jules R. Benjamin, 'The "Machadato" and Cuban Nationalism, 1928–1932', *Hispanic American Historical Review* 60 (1975), pp. 66–91; Ana Cairo, *El grupo minorista y su tiempo* (Havana, 1979); Ladislao González Carbajal, *El ala izquierda estudiantil y su época* (Havana, 1974); José A. Tabares del Real, *Guiteras* (Havana, 1973), and *La revolución del 30: Sus dos últimos años* (Havana, 1971);

Lionel Soto, *La revolución del 33,* 3 vols. (Havana, 1977); Jaime Suchliki, *University Students and Revolution in Cuba, 1920–1968* (Coral Gables, Fla., 1969), and Irwin F. Gellman, *Roosevelt and Batista: Good Neighbor Diplomacy in Cuba, 1933–1945* (Albuquerque, N.Mex., 1973).

3. CUBA, C. 1930–1959

Valuable chapters on Cuba treating the period from the *machadato* to the Revolution can be found in the following general studies: Hugh Thomas, *Cuba: The Pursuit of Freedom* (New York, 1971); Jaime Suchlicki, *Cuba: From Columbus to Castro* (3d ed., Washington, D.C., 1990); Jorge Dominguez, *Cuba: Order and Revolution* (Cambridge, Mass., 1978); Louis A. Pérez, Jr., *Cuba: Between Reform and Revolution* (New York, 1988); and Ramón Ruiz, *Cuba: The Making of a Revolution* (Amherst, Mass., 1968). Among the better recent general historical surveys published in Cuba are Oscar Pino Santos, *Historia de Cuba: Aspectos fundamentales* (Havana, 1964); Julio E. Le Riverend, *Historia de Cuba* (Havana, 1973), and Ministerio de Fuerzas Armadas Revolucionarias, *Historia militar de Cuba* (Havana, n.d.). A complete history of Cuba is contained in the ten-volume collaborative work supervised by Ramiro Guerra y Sánchez, *Historia de la nación cubana* (Havana, 1952). Also of some use is the three-volume work by Emeterio S. Santovenia and Raúl M. Shelton, *Cuba y su historia,* 3d ed. (Miami, 1966), and the five-volume study by José Duarte Oropesa, *Historiología cubana* (n.p., 1969–70), as well as Calixto C. Masó, *Historia de Cuba* (Miami, 1976), and Carlos Márquez Sterling, *Historia de Cuba, desde Colón hasta Castro* (New York, 1963). The two-volume anthology published under the auspices of the Grupo de Estudios Cubanos of the University of Havana, *La república neocolonial* (Havana, 1975–9), deals expertly with a variety of topics including labour, economic history, the armed forces, and the ABC revolutionary society. Another useful anthology dealing with the pre-Revolutionary period is the reprinted edition of Robert Freeman Smith (ed.), *Background to Revolution* (Huntington, N.Y., 1979). Wyatt Mac-Gaffey and Clifford R. Barnett, *Twentieth-Century Cuba* (New York, 1965), an invaluable reference work, contains much data on social, economic, political and cultural developments on the island. A similar format was used in the volume published by the Foreign Area Studies of American University, *Cuba: A Country Study* (2nd ed., Washington, D.C., 1985). Of some general value is Jaime Suchlicki, *Historical Dictionary of Cuba* (Metuchen, N.J., 1988). Another useful reference work, particularly for its wealth of statistical data, is José Alvarez Díaz et al., *A Study on Cuba* (Coral Gables, Fla., 1965). The most useful statistical compilation available is Susan Schroeder, *Cuba: A Handbook of Historical Statistics* (Boston, 1982).

Luis E. Aguilar, *Cuba 1933: Prologue to Revolution* (Ithaca, N.Y., 1972), remains one of the most balanced and judicious accounts of the *machadato* and the revolutionary tumult of the 1930s. For these years; see also Louis A. Pérez, Jr., *Cuba Under the Platt Amendment, 1902–1934* (Pittsburgh, Pa., 1986). The most complete study of the events of 1933, including an extensive treatment of the 1920s, is the three-volume work of Lionel Soto, *La revolución del 33*, 3 vols. (Havana, 1977). An excellent study of the eclipse of the revolutionary movement of the 1930s is found in José A. Tabares del Real, *La revolución del 30: Sus dos últimos años* (3rd ed., Havana, 1975). Also useful is Enrique de la Osa, *Crónica del año 33* (Havana, 1989). Of particular use are the first-person accounts of participants in the events of the 1930s. Ricardo Adam y Silva, *La gran mentira: 4 de septiembre de 1933* (Havana, 1947; 2nd ed., Miami, 1986) is a detailed account of the 'sergeants' revolt' by a former army officer. An anti-government officer account is found in Emilio Laurent, *De oficial a revolucionario* (Havana, 1941). Justo Carrillo, *Cuba 1933: estudiantes, yanquis y soldados* (Miami, 1985), is an important memoir of the government of one-hundred days as recounted by one of the leading student participants. Used with care, Gerardo Machado, *Memorias: Ocho años de lucha* (Miami, 1982), provides important insight into the late 1920s and early 1930s. Older memoirs are still of value. An adviser to Machado, Alberto Lamar Schweyer recounts the final days of the regime in *Como cayó el presidente Machado* (Madrid, 1941). The Secretary of War in the Cespedes government, Horacio Ferrer, treats the events of 1933 in key chapters of his memoir, *Con el rifle al hombro* (Havana, 1950). A useful first-person journalist account of 1933 is found in M. Franco Varona, *La revolución del 4 de septiembre* (Havana, 1934). A particularly useful first-person account of U.S. policy towards the Machado government during the early 1930s is provided in ambassador Harry Guggenheim's *The United States and Cuba* (New York, 1934).

Treatment of the 1930s through the 1950s is uneven. Raymond Leslie Buell, et al., *Problems of the New Cuba* (New York, 1935), remains as a landmark study of Cuba during the 1930s, dealing with virtually every aspect of Cuban national, provincial and municipal life. The International Bank for Reconstruction and Development, *Report on Cuba* (Baltimore, 1951), is similar in approach and scope for the 1940s and early 1950s. Similar in character if not in detail is Carlos M. Raggi Ageo, *Condiciones económicas y sociales de la república de Cuba* (Havana, 1944). Together these three studies are indispensable reference works for the period. Samuel Farber, *Revolution and Reaction in Cuba, 1933–1960* (Middletown, Conn., 1976), is an excellent study dealing with the period between the 1930s and the 1950s. A useful journalistic account of that period is Ruby Hart Phillips, *Cuba: Island of Paradox* (New York, 1959). National politics for these years are well treated in Ramón de Armas et al., *Los partidos burgueses en Cuba neocolonial, 1899–1952* (Havana, 1985). Enrique Vignier and Guillermo Alonso, *La corrupción política y administrativa en Cuba, 1944–1952* (Havana, 1952), is a documentary history of the Auténtico years. Also of some use for this period is the biography by Luis Conte Agüero, *Eduardo Chibás, el adalid de Cuba* (Mexico, 1955). By and large, however, the decade of the 1940s has been largely neglected.

This is not the case with the 1950s. The literature dealing with the revolutionary struggle against Batista is voluminous. Most of the monographic literature deals specifically with the politico-military aspects of the anti-Batista struggle. Some of the better English-language accounts include Ramón Bonachea and Marta San Martín, *The Cuban Insurrection* (New Brunswick, N.J., 1974); Herbert L. Matthews, *Revolution in Cuba* (New York, 1975); Robert Taber, *M-26, Biography of a Revolution* (New York, 1961); C. Fred Judson, *The Political Education of the Cuban Rebel Army, 1953–1963* (Boulder, Colo., 1984); and Mario Llerena, *The Unsuspected Revolution* (Ithaca, N.Y., 1986). One of the most detailed and moving accounts of the revolutionary struggle, concentrating on the last month of the war, is John Dorschner and Roberto Fabricio, *The Winds of December* (New York, 1980). Rolando E. Bonachea and Nelson P. Valdés, *Revolutionary Struggle, 1947–1958* (Cambridge, Mass., 1972), provides the texts of the major speeches and articles of Fidel Castro. One of the more comprehensive works dealing with the 1950s is José Barbeito, *Realidad y masificación: Reflexiones sobre la revolución cubana* (Caracas, 1964). José Suárez Núñez, *El gran culpable* (Caracas, 1963), and José A. Tabares de Real, *Ensayo de interpretación de la revolución cubana* (La Paz, 1960), are also useful for the 1950s. Among the better accounts of these years published in Cuba are Luis Emiro Valencia, *Realidad y perspectivas de la revolución cubana* (Havana, 1961); Mario Mencía, *La prisión fecunda* (Havana, 1980); and Tomás Toledo Batard, *La toma del poder* (Havana, 1989). For first-person government versions of these years, see Fulgencio Batista, *Cuba Betrayed* (New York, 1962); Florentino Rosell Leyva, *La verdad* (Miami, 1960); and Esteban Ventura Novo, *Memorias* (Mexico, 1961).

Numerous biographies of Fidel Castro also provide valuable accounts of these years. Among the most useful include Herbert Matthews, *Fidel Castro* (New York, 1969); Lionel Martin, *The Early Fidel: Roots of Castro's Communism* (Secaucus, N.J., 1978); Peter G. Bourne, *Fidel: A Biography of Fidel Castro* (New York, 1986); and Tad Szulc, *Fidel: A Critical Portrait* (New York, 1986). Of limited value is Georgie Anne Geyer, *Guerrilla Prince: The Untold Story of Fidel Castro* (Boston, 1991).

Much recent scholarship concentrates on specific aspects of Cuban history during these critical decades. Perhaps nowhere is the literature richer than in the area of relations between Cuba and the United States. An older but still useful study is Russell H. Fitzgibbon, *Cuba and the United States, 1900–1935* (Menasha, Wisc., 1935; rpt. New York, 1964). An excellent monograph which concludes with a treatment of the 1920s and 1930s is Jules R. Benjamin, *The United States and Cuba: Hegemony and Dependent Development, 1880–1934* (Pittsburgh, Pa., 1977). Irwin Gellman, *Roosevelt and Batista: Good Neighbor Diplomacy in Cuba, 1933–1945* (Albuquerque, N.Mex., 1973) examines the subsequent decade, with emphasis on diplomatic relations between both countries, recounted largely from the North American perspective and based principally on U.S. archival sources. The economic aspects of Cuba–U.S. relations are the principal focus of the balanced and thoughtful study by Robert F. Smith, *The United States and Cuba: Business and Diplomacy, 1917–1960* (New Haven, Conn., 1960). A more recent study dealing with the late 1950s is Morris H. Morley, *Imperial State and Revolution: The United States and Cuba, 1952–1986* (Cambridge, Eng., 1986). General accounts of Cuba–U.S. relations for these years can be found in Lester P. Langley, *The Cuban Policy of the United States: A Brief History* (New York, 1968); Michael J. Mazarr, *Semper Fidel: America and Cuba, 1776–1988* (Baltimore, 1988); Jules R. Benjamin, *The United States and the Origins of the Cuban Revolution* (Princeton, N.J., 1990); Louis A. Pérez, Jr., *Cuba and the United States: Ties of Singular Intimacy* (Athens, Ga., 1990). Three first-person accounts of U.S. diplomatic officials are also important sources for these years: Earl E. T. Smith, *The Fourth Floor* (New York, 1962); Philip W. Bonsal, *Cuba, Castro, and the United States* (Pittsburgh, Pa., 1971); and Wayne S. Smith, *The Closest of Enemies* (New York, 1987).

Other specialized monographs include Lowry Nelson, *Rural Cuba* (Minneapolis, 1950), an invaluable study that has been the point of departure for all subsequent research on life in the Cuban countryside. A useful study of the peasantry is found in Antero Regalado Falcón, *Las luchas campesinas en Cuba* (Havana, 1973). Louis A. Pérez, Jr., *Army and Politics in Cuba, 1898–1958* (Pittsburgh, Pa., 1975), treats the emergence of the armed forces in Cuban politics, as do the latter chapters of Frederico Chang, *El ejército nacional en la república neocolonial, 1899–1933* (Havana, 1981), and Rafael Fermoselle, *The Evolution of the Cuban Military, 1492– 1986* (Miami, 1987).

Among the most useful works on Cuban economic history are the two studies by Julio E. Le Riverend, *La República: Dependencia y revolución* (Havana, 1966), and *Historia económica de Cuba* (Havana, 1971). Also useful are Francisco López Segrera, *Cuba: Capitalismo dependiente y subdesarrollo (1510–1959)* (Havana, 1972), and the two works by Oscar Pino Santos, *El asalto a Cuba por la oligarquía financiera yanqui* (Havana, 1973), and *El imperialismo norteamericano en la economía de Cuba* (Havana, 1973). Another specialized economic study which contains useful chapters for the years 1930–58 is Jean Stubbs, *Tobacco on the Periphery* (London, 1985). Useful studies of labour include Carlos del Toro González, *Algunos aspectos económicos, sociales y políticos del movimiento obrero cubano (1933–1958)* (Havana, 1974); Evelio Jesús Tellería Toca, *Congresos obreros en Cuba* (Havana, 1973); and Mario Riera Hernández, *Historial obrero cubano, 1574–1965* (Miami, 1965).

Jaime Suchlicki, *University Students and Revolution in Cuba, 1920–1968* (Coral Gables, Fla., 1969), studies the role of students in national politics, as does Niurka Pérez Rojas, *El movimiento estudiantil universitario de 1934 a 1940* (Havana, 1975). A more specialized work dealing with student radicalism in the 1930s is Ladislao González Carbajal, *El ala izquierda estudiantil y su época* (Havana, 1974). Olga Cabrera and Carmen Almodobar compiled an important collection of documents related to student activism entitled *Las luchas estudiantiles universitarios, 1923–1934* (Havana, 1975).

4. CUBA SINCE 1959

Research on post-1959 Cuba has been handicapped because scholars in the country have concentrated on the years before 1959 and because field research in Cuba by outsiders on the post-1959 period has been rare and difficult. The secondary literature relies heavily on three types of sources: research on publications issued by the Cuban government, impressions of scholarly and other visitors to Cuba based on varying levels of systematic observation and research, and research on Cuban exiles. The last of these, however, focuses mostly on the exiles' integration into the United States rather than on generating systematic information about Cuba itself. The main scholarly journal for the study of contemporary Cuba is *Cuban Studies*, edited from 1970 to 1990 by Carmelo Mesa-Lago at the Center for Latin American Studies, University of Pittsburgh. Published twice a year until 1985, and once a year thereafter, it featured scholarly articles principally, though not exclusively, by social scientists on post-1959 Cuba. Each issue also offers the best and most complete bibliography of research on Cuba, conducted in or outside the country, on all fields. See also Ronald H. Chilcote and Cheryl Lutjens (eds.), *Cuba: 1953–1978: A Bibliographic Guide to the Literature*, 2 vols. (White Plains, N.Y., 1986), and also Louis A. Pérez, Jr., *Cuba: An Annotated Bibliography* (Westport, Conn., 1988). For bibliography on the years before 1970, see Nelson P. Valdés and Edwin Lieuwen, *The Cuban Revolution: A Research-Study Guide* (1959–1969) (Albuquerque, N.Mex., 1971). The best cartographic work is the joint publication by the Academia de Ciencias de Cuba and the Academia de Ciencias de la URSS, *Atlas nacional de Cuba* (Havana, 1970).

Many journals have been sponsored by the government, the party, the universities and the research institutes. *Cuba Socialista* covered political topics in depth and was the theoretical organ of the Cuban Communist Party until its discontinuation in the late 1960s, to reappear in December 1981. *Economía y Desarrollo*, published since the early 1970s by the economics faculty of the University of Havana, has covered economic topics within Cuba and abroad, including theoretical and empirical articles. *Pensamiento Crítico*, published in the 1960s until discontinued in 1970, covered philosophical and political topics. *Etnología y Folklore*, published briefly in the mid-1960s, covered topics in sociology and social anthropology.

The best contemporary social science research has been carried out by the government's Instituto Cubano de Investigaciones y Orientación de la Demanda Interna, under the leadership of Eugenio Rodríguez Balari. Its occasional publications, based on extensive systematic and random sampling, provide fascinating insights into Cuban life.

The research institutions linked to the party's Central Committee staff have been producing increasingly interesting work on international affairs, two of them working on matters pertaining to Cuba. The Centro de Estudios sobre América (CEA) began to issue occasional publications in the early 1980s; one of the best is the two-volume *El imperialismo norteamericano contemporáneo*. In 1983 it began to publish *Cuadernos de nuestra América* twice a year, especially helpful for Cuban views of U.S.–

Cuban relations and of the U.S. Cuban–American community. In 1981 the Centro de Investigaciones sobre la Economía Mundial (CIEM) began publishing *Temas de Economía Mundial*, a good source on Cuban foreign economic policy, especially on its economic relations with the Soviet Union and Eastern Europe. There have been some excellent public health journals, all entitled *Revista Cubana*, in various fields, including *Cirugía, Medicina, Medicina Tropical, Pediatría, Higiene y Epidemiología* and *Administración de Salud*.

Cuba's daily national-circulation newspapers have been *Granma* (morning) and *Juventud Rebelde* (afternoon). *Granma* was founded in late 1965 from the merger of the organs of the 26 of July Movement (*Revolución*) and of the PSP (*Noticias de Hoy*). *Granma* and its predecessors have been basic sources for primary research concerning contemporary Cuba. The speeches of Fidel Castro have often been published in full, as have been important speeches by other major figures. Cuba also publishes English and French weekly digest editions of the daily *Gramma*, at times drawing articles from other mass publications. The weekly digest helps the study of Cuba's international relations, but it is not sufficient for research on internal Cuban affairs. Translations tend to be good, but there are occasional serious errors. The best other mass-circulation source is the long-standing news magazine *Bohemia*, which covers a wide array of issues in some depth. Other general circulation publications for specialized research are *Verde Olivo* (military), *ANAP* (peasants), *Mujeres* (women), *Los Trabajadores* (workers), *Opina* (mass marketing), and *Con la Guardia en Alto* (Committees for the Defence of the Revolution), among others.

In late 1990 the Cuban government announced a 'special period in time of peace'. Among many other economic austerity measures, there was a severe curtailing in the availability of newsprint. Many of these publications have been suspended, discontinued or merged. It remains unclear which will continue to be published and which will reappear after having been temporarily suspended.

The most important statistical publication of the Cuban government has been the *Anuario estadístico de Cuba*, usually published with a two-year lag. Its inferior predecessor, the *Boletín*, was issued less regularly in the 1960s. The most common error in the use of the *Anuario* is to forget that its economic statistics are in current pesos and to forget as well that there has been inflation in Cuba, especially since the 1970s. It should be borne in mind that the educational statistics for the early 1960s refer only to public schools and that a substantial portion of the early increases in public school enrolment statistics result simply from the socialization of private schools. It should equally be noted that conceptual definitions in public health statistics have changed over time, and that malperforming sectors tend to be deleted from production statistics in subsequent years so that the *Anuario* gives a somewhat exaggerated impression of growth. The *Anuario* is rarely incorrect but it is often insufficient. For a thorough discussion of Cuban statistics during the 1960s, see Carmelo Mesa-Lago's 'Availability and Reliability of Statistics in Socialist Cuba', *Latin American Research Review* 4, no. 2 (1969). Mesa-Lago regularly reviews and evaluates the *Anuarios* in *Cuban Studies*. A valuable reference is Susan Schroeder's *Cuba: A Handbook of Historical Statistics* (Boston, 1982).

Three secondary works seek to be comprehensive in coverage. Hugh Thomas' *Cuba: The Pursuit of Freedom* (New York 1971) takes its coverage of historical developments up to the 1962 missile crisis, this being followed by a shorter discussion of events during the rest of that decade. Carmelo Mesa-Lago's *The Economy of Socialist Cuba: A Two-Decade Appraisal* (Albuquerque, N.Mex., 1981) discusses economic policy and performance, distribution, employment, social welfare and international economic factors. Jorge Domínguez, *Cuba: Order and Revolution* (Cambridge, Mass., 1978), focuses on politics and government. Some update is provided in Domínguez (ed.), *Cuba: Internal and International Affairs* (Beverly Hills, Calif., 1982). Good, short, general summaries on many topics are in Sandor Halebsky and John M. Kirk (eds.), *Cuba: Twenty-Five Years of Revolution: 1959 to 1984* (New York, 1985); in Sandor Halebsky and John M. Kirk (eds.), *Transformation and Struggle: Cuba Faces the 1990s* (New York, 1990); and in Sergio Roca (ed.), *Socialist Cuba: Past Interpretations and Future Challenges* (Boulder, Colo., 1988).

Other useful books on the economy are: Archibald Ritter, *The Economic Development of Revolutionary Cuba: Strategy and Performance* (New York, 1974), which gives a good coverage of the 1960s; Claes Brundenius, *Revolutionary Cuba: The Challenge of Economic Growth with Equity* (Boulder, Colo., 1984); and Alberto Recarte, *Cuba: Economía y poder* (1959–1980) (Madrid, 1980), which cover the 1970s as well. Interesting discussions of the Cuban economy cast in a wider social and political context from a Marxist perspective are to be found in James O'Connor, *The Origins of Socialism in Cuba* (Ithaca, N.Y., 1970), for the earlier years, and Arthur MacEwan, *Revolution and Economic Development in Cuba* (New York, 1981), for a later period. Cuba's leading academic economist, José Luis Rodriguez, publishes mostly through the CIEM; see his *Estrategia del desarrollo económico en Cuba* (Havana, 1990). A bibliographical and technical overview of the problems of estimating Cuba's economic growth rates is available from Carmelo Mesa-Lago and Jorge Pérez-López, 'A Study of Cuba's Material Product System: Its Conversion to the System of National Accounts, and Estimation of Gross Domestic Product Per Capita and Growth Rates', *World Bank Staff Working Papers*, no. 770 (Washington, D.C., 1985). A somewhat bitter but occasionally enlightening debate on this topic, between Mesa-Lago and Pérez-López versus Claes Brundenius and Andrew Zimbalist, appeared in *Comparative Economic Studies* in 1985 and 1986. See also Andrew Zimbalist, *Cuban Political Economy: Controversies in Cubanology* (Boulder, Colo., 1988). On economic measurement, see Jorge F. Pérez-López, *Measuring Cuban Economic Performance* (Austin, Tex., 1987), and also Andrew Zimbalist and Claes Brundenius, *The Cuban Economy: Measurement and Analysis of Socialist Performance* (Baltimore, 1989).

Four books have been published from the research project led by Oscar Lewis in Cuba in 1969–70, the only major field research conducted by outside scholars in revolutionary Cuba. The project ended when the Cuban government confiscated many of its tapes and notes and forced the Lewis group to leave. Their books provide much information on the lives of ordinary Cubans. Oscar Lewis, Ruth M. Lewis and Susan M. Rigdon are responsible for *Four Men* (Urbana, Ill., 1977), *Four Women* (Urbana, Ill., 1977), and *Neighbors* (Urbana, Ill., 1978), while Douglas Butterworth is responsible for *The People of Buena Ventura: Relocation of Slum Dwellers in Postrevolutionary Cuba* (Urbana, Ill., 1980).

Several books have captured important facets of Cuban politics and government policy in the 1960s. A superb discussion of the personal role and style of Fidel Castro is Edward Gonzalez, *Cuba Under Castro: The Limits of Charisma* (Boston, 1974). The best extended interview with Fidel Castro was published (along with excellent photographs) by Lee Lockwood in *Castro's Cuba, Cuba's Fidel* (New York, 1969). A thorough discussion of the factional politics of early revolutionary rule is provided by Andrés Suárez in *Cuba: Castroism and Communism* (Cambridge, Mass., 1967). A discussion of the radical politics of the 1960s appears in K. S. Karol, *Guerrillas in Power* (New York, 1970), and in René Dumont, *Cuba: Est-il socialiste?* (Paris, 1970), both rather critical; more sympathetic approaches to the regime's goals are given in Richard Fagen, *The Transformation of Political Culture in Cuba* (Stanford, 1969), and in Max Azicri, *Cuba: Politics, Economics and Society* (London, 1988). For an accessible overview, see

Juan del Aguila, *Cuba: Dilemmas of a Revolution* (Boulder, Colo., 1984). Valuable collections, covering several topics mostly dealing with Cuba in the 1960s, have been edited by Rolando Bonachea and Nelson P. Valdés, *Cuba in Revolution* (Garden City, N.Y., 1972); by Jaime Suchlicki, *Castro, Cuba and Revolution* (Coral Gables, Fla., 1972); and by Carmelo Mesa-Lago, *Revolutionary Change in Cuba* (Pittsburgh, Pa., 1971).

Other work on internal Cuban politics and political economy since the 1970s is, surprisingly, not very extensive. Special attention should be paid to the studies of Susan Eckstein, William LeoGrande and Nelson P. Valdés, some of which have appeared in *Cuban Studies*. A good, general collection on the 1980s is the seventh edition of Irving L. Horowitz's *Cuban Communism* (New Brunswick, N.J., 1989). On human rights and internal security, see the seven reports on Cuba issued by the Inter-American Commission on Human Rights of the Organization of American States (Washington, D.C., various years, most recently 1983), as well as the occasional reports from Amnesty International and Americas Watch. Important testimony is found in *El presidio político en Cuba comunista* (Caracas, 1982) and in Jorge Valls, *Twenty Years and Forty Days: Life in a Cuban Prison* (Washington, D.C., 1986). See also Luis Salas, *Social Control and Deviance in Cuba* (New York, 1979). There is little work on the Cuban armed forces. A useful manual is the U.S. Department of Defense, Directorate for Intelligence Research, Defense Intelligence Agency, *Handbook on the Cuban Armed Forces* (Washington, D.C., 1979), which is not classified. See also Rafael Fermoselle, *The Evolution of the Cuban Military: 1492–1986* (Miami, 1987), as well as his *Cuban Leadership after Castro: Biographies of Cuba's Top Generals* (Miami, 1987), and Jaime Suchlicki (ed.), *The Cuban Military under Castro* (Miami, 1989).

There has been an increase in publications concerning the international relations of the Cuban revolution. Eight edited collections gather much good work. They are Carmelo Mesa-Lago and Cole Blasier, *Cuba in the World* (Pittsburgh, Pa., 1979); Martin Weinstein; *Revolutionary Cuba in the World Arena* (Philadelphia, 1979); Carmelo Mesa-Lago and June Belkins, *Cuba in Africa* (Pittsburgh, Pa., 1982); Barry Levine, *The New Cuban Presence in the Caribbean* (Boulder, Colo., 1983); Sergio Díaz-Briquets, *Cuban Internationalism in Sub-Saharan Africa* (Pittsburgh, Pa., 1989); Instituto Superior de Relaciones Internacionales 'Raúl Roa', *De Eisenhower a Reagan* (Havana, 1987); Wayne S. Smith and Esteban Morales Domínguez, *Subject to Solution: Problems in Cuban–U.S. Relations* (Boulder, Colo., 1988); and Jorge I. Domínguez and Rafael Hernández, *U.S.–*

Cuban Relations in the 1990s (Boulder, Colo., 1989). See also: Carla A. Robbins, *The Cuban Threat* (New York, 1983); Lynn D. Bender, *Cuba vs. United States: The Politics of Hostility*, 2d rev. ed. (San Juan, 1981); W. Raymond Duncan, *The Soviet Union and Cuba* (New York, 1985); Pamela Falk, *Cuban Foreign Policy: Caribbean Tempest* (Lexington, Mass., 1985); H. Michael Erisman, *Cuba's International Relations: The Anatomy of a Nationalistic Foreign Policy* (Boulder, Colo., 1985); Wayne S. Smith, *The Closest of Enemies* (New York, 1987); Peter Shearman, *The Soviet Union and Cuba* (London, 1987); Morris H. Morley, *Imperial State and Revolution: The United States and Cuba, 1952–1986* (Cambridge, Eng., 1988); Damián J. Fernández, *Cuba's Foreign Policy in the Middle East* (Boulder, Colo., 1988); Francisco López Segrera, *Cuba: Política exterior y revolución (1959–88)* (Havana, 1988); Richard J. Payne, *Opportunities and Dangers of Soviet–Cuban Expansion* (Albany, N.Y., 1988); and Jorge I. Domínguez, *To Make a World Safe for Revolution: Cuba's Foreign Policy* (Cambridge, Mass., 1989).

An important source, monitoring U.S.–Cuban relations over time, and generating a great deal of information for primary research on this topic, has been the U.S. House of Representatives, Committee on Foreign Affairs, Subcommittee on Inter-American Affairs, through its published hearings records. The series of documents occasionally published by the Central Intelligence Agency, National Foreign Assessment Center, entitled *Communist Aid to Less Developed Countries of the Free World,* provides a useful, though at times controversial and incomplete, listing of the Cuban overseas presence. This organization also published two valuable reference aids in the late 1970s and early 1980s, namely, the *Directory of Officials of the Republic of Cuba,* and the *Chronology* (various years). All are unclassified.

There are some excellent sources on certain specialized topics. Seymour Menton's *Prose Fiction of the Cuban Revolution* (Austin, Tex., 1975) discusses literature and its social and political setting. On labour, see Maurice Zeitlin's *Revolutionary Politics and the Cuban Working Class* (New York, 1970), and Carmelo Mesa-Lago, *The Labor Sector and Socialist Distribution in Cuba* (New York, 1968). Juan and Verena Martínez Alier, in their *Cuba: Economía y sociedad* (Paris, 1972), are especially helpful on the early social, political and economic background of agrarian questions, and on gender and colour. For more recent years, see Carlos Moore, *Castro, the Blacks, and Africa* (Los Angeles, 1988). On religion, see John M. Kirk, *Between God and the Party: Religion and Politics in Revolutionary Cuba* (Gainesville, Fla., 1989). On government corruption, see *Case 1/1989: End of the Cuban Connection* (Havana, 1989).

INDEX